RELUCTANT WARRIOR
Ulysses S. Grant

> Born: April 27, 1822
> Died: July 23, 1885

A brilliant general who loathed war, a two-time President who scorned politics, a seeming failure in life who rose to the pinnacle of success only to have to fight a difficult battle against illness and financial ruin in his final years, Ulysses S. Grant is one of the truly fascinating figures in U. S. history. During the Union's darkest hours, Grant's victories in the West kept hope alive, and his defeat of Robert E. Lee brought the terrible conflict to an end. As President, his genius seemed to desert him, and he became an innocent pawn used by unscrupulous men for corrupt ends. Yet in later life his courage and honor restored him to his rightful place in our country's history.

BOOKS BY BOB & JAN YOUNG

Fiction

ACROSS THE TRACKS
GOOD-BYE, AMIGOS
SUNDAY DREAMER

Non-Fiction

50-40 OR FIGHT: The Story of the Oregon Territory
FORGED IN SILVER: The Story of the Comstock Lode
THE 49'ERS: The Story of the California Gold Rush
FRONTIER SCIENTIST: Clarence King
GUSHER: The Search for Oil in America
THE LAST EMPEROR:
The Story of Mexico's Fight for Freedom
OLD ROUGH AND READY: Zachary Taylor
PIKES PEAK OR BUST:
The Story of the Colorado Settlement
PLANT DETECTIVE: David Douglas
RELUCTANT WARRIOR: Ulysses S. Grant
SEVEN FACES WEST

RELUCTANT WARRIOR

Ulysses S. Grant

by Bob & Jan Young

JULIAN MESSNER NEW YORK

Published by Julian Messner
a division of Simon & Schuster, Inc.
1 West 39th Street, New York, N.Y. 10018
All Rights Reserved

Copyright, © 1971 by Jan Young

Printed in the United States of America

ISBN 0-671-32439-X   Cloth Trade
        0-671-32440-3   MCE

Library of Congress Catalog Card No. 77-160305

CONTENTS

I	The Boy Who Loved Horses	7
II	Cadet Sam Grant	21
III	Love and War	32
IV	On to Mexico City	48
V	Between Wars	60
VI	Back in Harness	71
VII	The Pendulum of War	87
VIII	Hero of Vicksburg	100
IX	Top Command	111
X	The Final Blow	123
XI	"Let Us Have Peace"	136
XII	The New President	147
XIII	Second Term	157
XIV	Ambassador to the World	167
XV	The Last Battle	177
	Suggested Further Readings	185
	Index	187

Chapter 1

The Boy Who Loved Horses

Summertime was circus time in southwestern Ohio. Entertainments were few and mostly homemade in the rural United States in the 1830s, but during the long summer months hardly a county seat west of the Alleghenies was so small that it was not visited by at least one traveling circus, with its motley collection of acrobats, jugglers, swordswallowers and freaks. What these traveling shows lacked in professional acts, they often made up in audience participation, offering a five-dollar prize to any local youth who could stay three rounds with the circus strong man or hang on for three circles of the ring on a trick pony.

Georgetown, the county seat of Brown County, Ohio, was no exception that summer of 1833. Since early morning wagons and buggies had been rolling into town where a flapping canvas tent had been set up in a vacant field. The audience had already been entertained by the antics of three large monkeys, a juggler, acrobats and a fire swallower. Now it was time for the trick pony. Two youths in their late teens tried their luck. The audience screamed encouragement, then groaned in disappointment as each was thrown.

While the last rider was picking himself up, a small, stocky

RELUCTANT WARRIOR: ULYSSES S. GRANT

boy of eleven with sandy hair and a round, serious face edged closer to the ring. "You show 'em, Lyss," a younger companion encouraged in a piping voice.

The ringmaster grinned confidently at the newcomers. "Getting a better look, boys, or do you fancy you can earn that five dollars?"

Without speaking, the stocky boy slipped under the ropes, indicating that he wanted to try for the money. A roustabout caught up the pony, another helped the boy to its slippery back and the ringmaster signaled for the animal to be turned loose.

The pony took off at a gallop, ground its heels into the dirt and came to an abrupt stop, whirled in a circle and shot off again. The small boy wrapped chunky arms around its neck and hung on.

"C'mon, Lyss!" his companion shrieked.

As the pony completed the first circle of the ring, the ringmaster's smile faded. A crack of his whip sent the animal into a new frenzy of dashes, turns and sudden stops.

The audience began stamping and shouting.

"That's the way!"

"Ride 'em, boy!"

"You show 'em, Lyss!"

The ringmaster frowned. Circuses were not in business to lose money. As boy and pony came around the ring a second time, he seized one of the performing monkeys and tossed it onto the rider's back. Chattering and screeching, the monkey scrambled to the boy's shoulders and clamped its hairy arms around his head. Between shrieks of encouragement, the audience was convulsed with laughter. The boy gave no sign that he heard. As though unaware of the unwelcome, clawing passenger on his back, he concentrated on completing the last circle of the ring.

Seeing he was beaten, the ringmaster motioned for the pony

The Boy Who Loved Horses

to be stopped and begrudgingly handed over the money. As the boy accepted the prize and slipped away in the crowd, some of the audience called their congratulations. Others turned away, less vocal in their admiration. They knew that for months to come Jesse Grant, the boy's father, would be boasting about this exploit as one more proof of his son's superior talents. In the opinion of most of the townspeople of Georgetown, eleven-year-old Ulysses Grant had only one recognizable talent—his ability to handle horses. The lad was too shy and backward, they felt, ever to live up to the brilliant future his father was continually predicting for him.

Hiram Ulysses Grant was born on April 27, 1822, in a two-room cottage in the small village of Point Pleasant, Ohio. From the house, which stood on a bluff next door to his father's tannery, he could look across the Ohio River to the green trees of the Kentucky shoreline. When Jesse Grant had come west in 1798, this country had been the frontier. Now churning steamboats plied the river on a regular run between Pittsburgh and New Orleans. Smaller keelboats and barges moved by in a steady procession, bound for the burgeoning trade center of Cincinnati, twenty-five miles downstream. Though this section of southwestern Ohio was still sparsely settled, only a small proportion of the new settlers who came down the river each spring in flotillas of flatboats stopped in Ohio to build their homes. The frontier had moved farther west now, beyond the Mississippi River to the rich new prairie lands opened up by the Louisiana Purchase of 1803.

Of Scottish origin, the Grant family traced their ancestry back to a Matthew Grant who had settled in Massachusetts in 1630. Ulysses' great-grandfather and a great-uncle had died in the French and Indian Wars and his grandfather, Captain Noah Grant, had served in the Revolutionary War. An affable but improvident man, Noah Grant had drifted slowly west with his large family from Connecticut to Pennsylvania and on to Ohio. In 1804, on the death of his second wife, the family had broken up and young Jesse Grant had been on his own.

For a few years Jesse worked for neighboring farmers. He then decided to learn the tanner's trade. Most of his apprenticeship was learned working for an older brother, who already owned a tannery in Kentucky; but for one year he worked and lived with another tanner, Owen Brown, whose fifteen-year-old-son, John Brown, was already becoming a fanatical abolitionist. Though Jesse did not embrace John Brown's fanaticism, he also was opposed to slavery. When he had a chance to go into business for himself at Point Pleasant, where a storekeeper was looking for a partner to set up a tannery, Jesse told people that the reason he decided to move from Kentucky to the Ohio side of the river was because he "would not own slaves, and would not live among people who did."

The Point Pleasant business prospered and by 1821 Jesse was sufficiently out of debt to marry Hannah Simpson, the daughter of a local farmer. To most people the couple seemed oddly mismatched. Jesse was ambitious and driving. A nonstop talker, he bombarded local newspapers with letters expressing his political opinions and loved to debate and argue. In contrast, Hannah was retiring and quiet almost to the point of eccentricity. Yet they seemed to complement each other and it was a happy marriage. In time they would have six children, three boys and three girls, but it was Jesse's first born who was his special pride. From the day of the infant's birth, Jesse was unshakable in his belief that this first child was destined for greatness.

Even the choice of the infant's name became a matter of grave concern. For a month the baby went unnamed. Finally, Jesse and Hannah took the infant to the Simpson farm where everyone in the family wrote his selection on a slip of paper.

There were two votes for Ulysses, after the Greek hero who had defeated the Trojans by means of the wooden horse, but only one apiece for an assortment of other names. Jesse finally chose Hiram, the choice of Grandfather Simpson, as the baby's first name, with Ulysses as his middle name. Since Ulysses had been Hannah's preference, he soon became simply "Lyss" to her and most of his friends.

When Ulysses was a year old, the family moved to Georgetown, twenty-five miles away. It was no larger than Point Pleasant, but as the county seat, Jesse felt it promised greater growth. From Tom L. Hamer, a young politician who was currently justice of peace, Jesse purchased a parcel of land at the corner of Main and Water Streets, a block from the town square. On the corner he built a brick currier shop where he sold his leather. Behind this was the tannery itself, with its lime vats where the hair was loosened from the hides, the beam room where they were scraped and other vats containing sulfuric acid and the tanbark emulsion that completed the cure. In addition, there were open sheds for storing the oak bark and a grinding mill where it was pulverized. Across the street from the currier shop, Jesse built a brick house, adding rooms and a second story over the years until it became one of the most substantial homes for miles around.

Because of their mutual interest in politics, Jesse Grant and Tom Hamer became immediate friends. Other Georgetown residents were more reserved in their acceptance of the newcomer. Georgetown had been settled largely by Southerners. Jesse had the saving grace of being a Democrat, but he was antislavery, a Methodist and a teetotaler, and his excessive drive and ambition were alien to many of his neighbors, who preferred a more leisurely pace of life. But the tannery furnished jobs and new industry. As business prospered, Jesse bought up neighboring forest lands where he could cut the oaks needed for the tanning process. Teams of horses were required to haul the wood and to operate the grinding mill. To keep the animals productive when not in use at the tannery, Jesse rented them out for local draying jobs and eventually expanded this to the operation of a livery stable. Later, to secure a steady supply of hides, he opened his own slaughterhouse.

Aside from having the same reddish brown hair and blue eyes, young Ulysses showed little resemblance to his father. Jesse was a rangy man, standing well over six feet tall, while the boy was small for his age and inclined to be plump. Instead of being bombastic and outgoing like his father, Ulysses was self-contained and as untalkative as his mother. While still a toddler, he loved to hold the teams of those who came to do business with his father. In their own stables, he crawled unafraid in and out between the big feet of the horses. One day a neighbor came screaming to Hannah that the infant was sitting underneath one of the horses playing with its tail. Unruffled, Hannah did not bother to look up from her cooking. "Lyss has a way with horses," she said calmly.

Jesse encouraged this interest by placing the toddler on the horses' backs as he led them to water at nearby White Oak Creek. By the time he was five, Ulysses was driving the teams alone for their noon and evening watering, usually standing erect on one of the animals' backs.

That same year, Jesse decided it was time for his son to start school. There were no public schools in Ohio in those days, only "subscription schools." The parents in a town would get together and pledge several dollars a semester for each child they wished taught. When enough pledges were secured to provide a salary of about ten dollars a month, a teacher would be hired. The pupils crowded into the one-room schoolhouse ranged in age from five-year-olds like Ulysses to hulking twenty-year-old farmhands. Lessons were learned by rote and pounded in to the accompaniment of birch-rod switchings. In later years, classmates recalled that, if Ulysses did not get as many switching as the others, it was not due to his brillance but because he was so quiet that sometimes the teacher hardly noticed that he was there. He was good in arithmetic and could calculate sums in his head as quickly as on paper, but in other subjects he was only fair. He particularly disliked composition and public recitation. The only occasion on which he actively rebelled in class was when one teacher instituted a program of public speaking. Ulysses stammered through two speeches, while even his classmates writhed in sympathy, then announced flatly that he would never get up in class and make a speech again.

On the playground he was inclined to be a loner. He disliked team sports. When he did participate, it was in riding, swimming or wrestling, in which he could compete alone. He became proficient enough with a gun to take first place in a Fourth of July shooting contest, but he refused to go hunting with the other boys. He could not stand the thought of killing any live creature and had such a distaste for the sight of blood that he would not eat wild game or touch any kind of meat unless it was cooked to a crisp. Another eccentricity in which his family indulged him, was his dislike for music. Not only was he so tone deaf that he found it hard to distinguish one melody from another, but musical notes actually seemed to hurt his ears, or so he convinced his father, so that on Sundays, when his parents attended church with his younger sisters and brothers, he was actually allowed to remain home. Later as a grown man, he amused his friends by claiming that in all his life he had only learned to recognize two tunes, adding, "One was 'Yankee Doodle,' and the other was not."

In spite of these peculiarities, he was well liked by his classmates, for nothing ever seemed to upset him and he got along with everyone. His ability as a horseman was the envy of most of the boys his age. By the time he was eight he was already driving teams hauling oak to the tannnery by himself, and his skill in gentling and training colts was known for miles around. On horseback he seemed to lose his shyness—his favorite arena for breaking colts was the town square, where he could be certain of an appreciative audience.

He also acquired a reputation for scrupulous honesty, naïvely expecting the same treatment in return. One day a farmer asked Ulysses to deliver an important letter to a friend twenty miles away, offering the use of his own horse for the ride. Once Ulysses was mounted, the farmer slyly mentioned that he had never been able to teach his horse to pace. Just as the farmer had anticipated, when Ulysses returned from the long, hot trip the horse was pacing beautifully. But when the farmer let it leak out in town that the letter had only been a ruse to get the horse trained, Ulysses was so crushed by this dishonesty that he refused to train a horse for anyone else again.

Once his honesty even became a town joke. Ulysses admired a horse owned by a farmer who frequently stopped by the tannery. When the owner asked twenty-five dollars for the animal, Jesse protested that it was too much. After the man had gone, Ulysses continued to argue and plead and Jesse finally relented. Giving the boy twenty-five dollars, he sent him out to the farm to make the deal himself, cagily instructing him to offer twenty dollars first, raise that to $22.50, and only pay twenty-five dollars if absolutely necessary.

Ulysses nodded that he understood, but when he reached the home of the prospective seller, he blurted out, "My father gave me twenty-five dollars to buy the horse, but he said I was to offer you only twenty dollars first, then twenty-two fifty after that." Needless to say, he paid the full price. The story was told and retold in town, particularly by those who had become annoyed with Jesse's boasting about the boy's cleverness. Others who liked the quiet boy and knew how often he was embarrassed by his father's bragging, said the incident only proved his basic honesty.

The same distaste for blood that prevented Ulysses from enjoying hunting extended to the tannery, a malodorous, gory place with its stinking vats and rows of blood- and flesh-encrusted hides. When he was assigned the job of feeding bark into the grinding mill, Ulysses would skip off to the town square and hire another boy to do his work, then take out one of the teams of horses and look up a draying job to pay off his substitute. By the time he was nine, he was making business trips alone as far as Cincinnati for his father and driving livery-stable customers to towns thirty and forty miles away.

The year 1833 was a particularly eventful one for eleven-year-old Ulysses. With his father he made the trip by steamer to Maysville, Kentucky, to bring back his widowed Aunt Margaret and her five children to live at Georgetown. One of the cousins, Johnny Marshall, was only a little bit younger than Ulysses. Best of all, Johnny willingly took over the job of feeding the grinding mill, leaving Ulysses free to work in the livery stable.

For all his outward seriousness, Ulysses indulged in his share of boyish pranks. Shortly after the Marshalls came to live at Georgetown, Ulysses bet his cousin a handful of marbles that he could jump twenty-five feet in a single leap. Certain he had a sure thing, Johnny accepted the offer. Grinning, Ulysses led the way to a high bank along the creek and with a wild whoop leaped off the edge, landing nearly thirty feet below in soft mud up to his hips.

That same summer there was an outbreak of Asiatic cholera in Cincinnati. Determined that his family should be protected if the disease spread to Georgetown, Jesse brought home two huge demijohns: one filled with an evil-tasting medicine, the other with blackberry cordial for the relief of the diarrhea which frequently accompanied the illness. Many hot afternoons that summer Ulysses escorted his youthful friends down to the family cellar where he gave each a small mouthful of the vile medicine. All immediately spat it on the ground in disgust, after which he treated them to a much larger and more enjoyable swig of the cordial.

The summer that Ulysses was twelve, Jesse got the contract for supplying lumber for a new jail, a job that required several months of cutting huge logs and hauling them into town. Ulysses offered to do all the hauling if his father would purchase a huge work horse named Dave, which he had long admired. Jesse agreed to the purchase of Dave, but doubted that Ulysses was strong enough to keep up with the hauling, and hired a man to ride along with him. Before the first week was over, the man quit, complaining that there was nothing for him to do. After that Ulysses worked alone, driving to the forest where the wood choppers loaded the wagon, then hauling the huge loads back into town for two or three trips each day. One morning Jesse was startled to see him unharnessing the team after only one load. "Why are you quitting so early?" he asked.

"The woodchoppers weren't there today," Ulysses replied. "I loaded all the logs left from yesterday, but there won't be any more wood until tomorrow."

Jesse looked from the mountain of logs to his small son. "If the choppers weren't there, how did you get the logs onto the wagon?"

Ulysses shrugged. "Dave and I did it." He explained that he had looked around until he found a half-fallen tree slanting out from the ground. Driving the wagon under the trunk, he had unhitched Dave, fastened chains to the logs and, using the big horse's strength, dragged the logs one at a time up the slanting trunk to where they could be dropped into the wagon. Jesse lost no time in telling this new story around town.

That summer a professor who claimed to be a noted phrenologist stopped in Georgetown. Phrenology, the art of predicting a person's character from the bumps on his head, was the rage at that time. As soon as Jesse heard of the visitor, he rushed Ulysses to him. The phrenologist ran his hands through the boy's thick hair, feeling every contour of his skull, then announced in a solemn voice: "A remarkable head. This lad could grow up to be President some day." It was a common prediction, made by all phrenologists for doting parents, but Jesse took it literally and again his boasting knew no bounds.

If Ulysses was to amount to something, he would need a better education than that afforded by the "subscription school." That fall Jesse sent Ulysses to live with other relatives in Maysville, Kentucky. Aside from conquering his fear of public speaking enough to join the debating society, Ulysses found the Maysville school little different from the one at home. He was relieved when he returned home the following summer to learn that his father could not afford to send him back.

In 1837 the country was suffering from a financial panic and depression. The steps leading up to the depression had changed Jesse Grant's politics and cost him one of his closest friends. For years Jesse and Tom Hamer had been friends and Jesse had supported Hamer in his election to state office and later to Congress. As fellow Democrats, they had shared a mutual enthusiasm for Andrew Jackson when he was elected for his first term in 1828; but by the time Jackson began his second term, Jesse had become disenchanted with his former idol. He particularly distrusted Jackson's fiscal policy, which he believed could lead to irresponsible speculation and a possible panic. Breaking with the Democratic Party, Jesse turned to the new Whig Party being formed by Henry Clay. After the resulting bitter quarrel, Hamer and Jesse stopped speaking to each other.

The Grants were too solidly prosperous to be more than

temporarily hurt by the brief depression, but that fall Ulysses attended school in Georgetown again. The following summer, when his father informed him that the time had come for him to start learning the tanner's trade, the two came as close as they ever had to a serious quarrel. Ulysses said he would obey, but only until he was twenty-one when he would leave home.

Jesse was stunned. He knew Ulysses disliked the tannery, but he had not realized his hatred was so intense. "What do you want to do with your life then?" he asked.

Unfortunately, at sixteen Ulysses had not given this much thought. "I guess I'd like to be a farmer ... or maybe a trader on the river," he offered.

For once in his life Jesse Grant did not argue, but he was far from pleased. To farm required land. By now Granfather Simpson had died, but the small section of land that had been Hannah's inheritance was already leased out. As for being a river trader, Jesse considered them a roistering, dissolute lot. That fall when Ulysses returned to school, Jesse sent him to the Presbyterian Academy at the nearby town of Ripley.

Already a new idea was forming in Jesse's mind. There was one place where his son could get an excellent education and a free one to boot. That was at the United States Military Academy at West Point. In recent years three local boys had received appointments to the academy: the Ammen brothers, sons of the newspaper editor, and Bart Bailey, son of the doctor. Once Ulysses was off to Ripley, Jesse wrote to Senator Thomas Morris of Ohio, asking for an appointment. The Senator replied that he had no appointments available, but had looked into the matter and learned there would be an opening very soon in Jesse's own district if he would write to Congressman Hamer. It was a difficult decision, but getting Ulysses into West Point was becoming an obsession with Jesse. He swallowed his pride and wrote to Hamer.

In 1838 when Ulysses came home for the Christmas holi-

The Boy Who Loved Horses

days, his father had a surprise for him. "I think you're going to receive the appointment," Jesse announced.

"What appointment?" Ulysses asked.

Jesse beamed. "Why, to West Point, of course."

"I won't go!" Ulysses declared.

Jesse's blue eyes were cool behind his metal-rimmed glasses. "I think you will," he said sternly.

As Ulysses wrote years later in his *Memoirs*, "With that, I thought I would, too."

Ulysses had no desire to go to West Point, even less to be a soldier. At the close of the holidays he returned to Ripley comforted by the memory of his father's quarrel with Congressman Hamer. Surely the Congressman would refuse the recommendation.

He was mistaken. By now Hamer regretted the fight with his old friend. Jesse's letter reached Washington, D.C., at the close of Hamer's term as he was packing to return to Georgetown. What better way to patch up their old differences than to recommend Jesse Grant's son to the vacancy just created by the failure and dismissal of Bart Bailey from the academy? The only trouble was that Hamer had forgotten the boy's full name. Then he remembered that Ulysses' mother had been a Simpson. Hastily, Hamer wrote a letter to the Secretary of War, recommending Ulysses Simpson Grant for an appointment to West Point.

In March Ulysses received word at Ripley that he was to come home at once. The appointment had been approved and he was leaving for New York in May. He returned home with mixed emotions. His father could hardly contain himself with pride, and townspeople and friends filled the house to congratulate him, but his misgivings were not helped when he learned that his appointment had only been possible because of the dismissal of Bart Bailey, who had been his friend. Dr. Bailey was so ashamed that he had disowned Bart and forbidden him to ever come home again. Ulysses hid his tormenting doubts. He had never been a particularly good scholar. What if he failed also? Would his father disown him?

There was much to be done. Purchases had to be made: a rugged, serviceable suit, heavy square-toed shoes that were the best available in the Cincinnati stores and a sturdy new trunk. Cousin Johnny helped him pound in his initials into the trunk with brass tacks. H. U. G. Ulysses remembering hearing one of the Ammen boys tell about the hazing given new plebes for any humorous peculiarity. "HUG," that would never do. When his father wasn't looking, he switched the tacks to read UHG. On May 15, 1839, with the trunk in the wagon behind him, the altered initials carefully turned so that no one could see them, he set off for Ripley where he was to catch the river steamer. He still didn't want to go to West Point.

Chapter II

Cadet Sam Grant

The journey to West Point would have been the adventure of young Ulysses Grant's life, if it had not been for its dreaded destination. As the paddle-wheeler churned upriver and into western Pennsylvania, Grant clung to the rail by day eagerly taking in all the sights. But at night he lay in his bunk, indulging in a boyish fantasy where the steamer suffered a collision in midstream and he was injured seriously enough to become ineligible for the academy without being handicapped for life.

No such fortuitous accident occurred. At the end of three days the steamer docked safely at Pittsburgh and Grant transferred to a canal boat that carried him on to Harrisburg. Here, trying to assume the nonchalance of a seasoned traveler, he boarded a railway train for the first time in his life and was carried east at the breathtaking speed of twelve miles an hour to Philadelphia. After a week's visit with some of his mother's relatives, he continued on to New York City for a couple days more of sightseeing before boarding the Hudson River steamer that carried him upstream to the gray stone buildings and cropped green parade grounds of West Point.

On May 29, 1839, he presented himself at the office of the adjutant and signed the register "Ulysses Hiram Grant," to conform to the initials on his trunk. The clerk compared the signature with the list forwarded by the War Department. "Sorry, we have no appointment for any Ulysses Hiram Grant," he said curtly.

Grant's brief hope for a reprieve was shattered as the clerk consulted the list again. "But we do have appointments for Elihu Grant of New York and Ulysses Simpson Grant of Ohio."

When Grant explained that he was the Ohio appointee and an error must have been made in his name, he had his first encounter with governmental red tape. Civilians and even Congressmen might make errors but not the Army. It would require an official order from the War Department to change his name. Grant considered the problem; then, never having been inclined to argument, he signed the register again as Ulysses Simpson Grant, the name that would remain with him for the rest of his life.

A sophomore was summoned to lead Grant to his quarters. Outside the office the last names and initials of the new arrivals had been posted on a bulletin board. A group of first classmen, looking awesomely smart and superior in their long gray coats, skin-tight white pants and flat gigtop hats, were gathered around it studying the names for peculiarities. A tall redhead, Will Sherman, was the first to make the discovery. "U. S. Grant!" he hooted. "Uncle Sam Grant!"

Propelled forward by his grinning sophomore escort, Grant managed a fumbling salute. Instead of a tall, lanky youth resembling the popular caricature of Uncle Sam, the upperclassmen saw a stubby, moon-faced boy weighing 117 pounds and standing five foot one, just one inch above the academy's minimum height requirement.

The disparity was so great they howled with laughter. Their eyes swept on to Grant's plain, rough-textured suit and heavy shoes, as broad at the toes as at the heels, that set him apart from the more fashionably dressed boys from the Eastern and Southern States. "Country Sam" someone else suggested.

Sherman shook his head. "Uncle Sam," he persisted. The nickname was to stick throughout Grant's academy years, though in time it would mercifully be shortened to plain Sam. "A more unpromising boy never entered the Military Academy," was the verdict of William Tecumseh Sherman, who had endured the nickname of Cump in his own plebe year.

The hilarity over Grant's name was only the beginning of the hazing, which continued those next weeks as the appointees prepared for their entrance exams. "Salute. . . . Say, 'Sir.' . . . Eyes front. . . . Remember you're animals, things, not human beings. . . . Repeat after me: 'I AM AN ANIMAL.' " On and on it went, with sophomores popping into the barracks day and night to rouse the newcomers to attention and to endure the taunts. Because of his small stature and clumsiness, Grant drew more than his share, but unlike many of his companions, he never appeared upset or flustered and shrugged it off with good humor.

A greater torture in Grant's opinion was the drill practice which began the next morning and continued daily. Walking with the rolling gait of a natural horseman, he was unbelievably clumsy on the drill field. He had difficulty picking up the beat of the drums, which added to the handicap. Most of his first weeks were spent hopping from one foot to another trying to keep in step, and for the rest of his life he would thoroughly hate all military drill.

In spite of his shyness, Grant's easygoing disposition slowly began to win him friends. Everyone admired the way he stoically stood up to the hazing except for one hulking appointee, the son of an army colonel, who was thoroughly spoiled by the academy officers who were helping him prepare for the exams. He carried his arrogance over to the barracks, and during squad drill, he particularly delighted in elbowing Grant out of line. One day after several warnings to quit shoving, Grant turned and, with a bland expression that showed no trace of anger, hit the bully such a resounding blow in his stomach that he knocked him flat. After that, Grant's standing rose considerably among his peers.

As the appointees drilled, crammed and sweated out the weeks until the July exams, the upperclassmen indulged in a favorite academy pastime of placing odds on those who they thought would survive. Most heavily favored were the boys from the East because of the superiority of their preparatory schools. Next, came the boys from the Southern states. Though their schools were considered inferior, they were inclined to be more poised and skilled in social graces and in many instances had an added factor of incentive. While most of the Eastern boys planned to leave the Army for more lucrative careers in civilian life, once they had served their required years after graduation, a proportionately high percentage of Southerners hoped to make the Army a lifetime career.

Lowest on the scale were the appointees from the Western states, who were handicapped by their lack of social graces as well as their backwoods schooling. Statistics bore out the ratings. Of all the appointees it was not unusual for from 30 to 50 percent to fail the entrance exams. Of those who were admitted, another 50 percent would not make it through the entire four years. But in the case of the boys from the Western states these odds were nearly doubled.

Fortunately, Grant seemed unaware of the odds against him. As the time for the exams drew closer, he appeared to be the least nervous of all the candidates. Philosophically, he had decided to do his best, then wait to see what happened before he started worrying. When the day finally arrived when he had to stand at attention before the blackboard and answer the questions thrown at him by the thirteen examining officers, he found the test easier than he had anticipated. In mathematics he shone, and in the other subjects he managed well enough that out of the ninety boys who took the exams that year, he was among the sixty who passed.

With the exams behind them, the new plebes were outfitted with uniforms and sent out in the field to the summer encampment, where they would remain until the start of classes in September. At the encampment the hazing continued, with the plebes carrying water, chopping wood, putting up tents and doing all the manual labor. Grant's country background stood him in good stead and he did not find the work particularly hard.

Though the plebes were forbidden to make friends outside their own class, the encampment gave them a chance to watch the upperclassmen in action. There was much speculation as to which ones would have the most brilliant military careers. Among the seniors the ebullient Sherman and his best friend, solemn George H. Thomas, were the favorites, with the eagle-eyed Virginian, Richard S. Ewell, a close third. Among the sophomores, with whom they had more contact, William S. "Rosey" Rosecrans was considered the smartest; two Southerners, Don Carlos Buell and Earl Van Dorn, were predicted to go far if they learned to curb their high spirits; and tall, slender James Longstreet was thought the most military in bearing.

Captain Charles F. Smith, the commandant of cadets, was considered the most dashing of all the academy officers, until the memorable day when General Winfield Scott, supreme commander of the U. S. Army, visited the encampment. A hero of the War of 1812, Scott was such a "spit and polish" general that he had been given the nickname "Old Fuss and Feathers." As he appeared before the cadets, his towering six foot four frame resplendent in full-dress uniform, Grant was so impressed that he could not help wondering for a moment how it would feel to stand in the general's shoes and know you were the top man of the entire army. But as Grant wrote years later in his *Memoirs,* the thought was only fleeting. Two months at West Point had reinforced his conviction that he did not want to become a professional soldier. As yet he had no definite plans for the future, only that if he managed to survive the four years at West Point, he was going to serve his required time and resign as soon as possible.

In September the cadets returned to West Point for the start of classes. Grant's roommate was Rufus Ingalls, a small, lively boy with an irrepressible sense of humor, with whom he shared a small room on the fourth floor of the North Barracks. The principal studies that semester were algebra, which Grant liked and found easy, and French, which he disliked and studied just enough to scrape by.

By now Grant was familiar with the academy demerit system. At the start of each year each cadet was allowed a maximum of two hundred. Demerits, ranging from one for minor infractions to ten for the most serious offenses, were chalked up for every breach of military discipline. If at any time before the end of the year a cadet reached the total of two hundred, it meant instant dismissal. Like most of his classmates, Grant had no expectation of matching the unbeaten record of brilliant young Robert E. Lee who had graduated from the academy ten years before without a single demerit having been charged against him. But most of the fifty-nine demerits Grant received that first year were for minor infractions, usually sloppiness of dress, unpolished shoes, missing buttons, raveled gloves. His single major offense, one that cost him eight demerits and confinement to his room for a week, was for failure to attend church. Unlike many of his fellow plebes, Grant never wrote home complaining about the plain food or hazing. But he did write to a cousin protesting this punishment and pointing out that, since he was a Methodist and the cadets were forced to attend Episcopalian service, he considered the rule undemocratic.

Cadet Sam Grant

In 1839 Congress was already being wracked with the dissension between the North and South that would lead eventually to the Civil War, particularly as new states were admitted to the Union and it had to be decided whether they would be slave or free. Because the cadets came from all sections of the country, they were forbidden to discuss politics, but that winter Grant found himself avidly following one debate that was going on in Congress. The United States maintained only a very small standing army at that time. Because so many West Point graduates resigned from the service immediately upon completing their required four years, a bill had been introduced into Congress to do away with the academy entirely. Grant prayed that the bill would pass so that he would be free to return home. To his disappointment it failed, and a few weeks later, when he passed his January exams, his probational period ended.

Grant made only one more attempt to escape the academy. Nearby Benny Haven's tavern was off limits to the cadets. Though being caught there could result in severe punishment or even dismissal, some of the more rambunctious cadets still slipped away occasionally. The tavern itself had no interest for Grant, but one afternoon in a fit of pique at the whole military establishment he put on his full uniform and set out for the tavern, going out of his way to salute every officer he saw in hopes of being caught and discharged. To his chagrin, he was so brazen that the officers assumed he was on a legitimate errand and he did not draw even a reprimand.

After that incident, Grant seemed to abandon hope of escaping and settled down to serve out the next eight years. In June when his plebe year ended, he ranked twenty-seventh in a class of sixty, a position in the middle from which he would vary little during the remaining three years.

Cadets were only allowed one leave home at the end of their sophomore year, so that summer Grant returned to the encampment. Perhaps because of the memories of his own plebe year, he took little part in the hazing of the new appointees. They were a rather undistinguished freshman class, a Southern boy with the romantic name of Simon Bolivar Buckner showing the most dash.

Grant found his second year at the academy more enjoyable than the first. That year classes in horsemanship were introduced for the first time as part of the cadets' training. Though only a sophomore, within a short time Grant was recognized as the best horseman at West Point. That year he also was allowed to make friends outside his own class and James Longstreet, who shared his enthusiasm for riding, became a close friend. Grant enjoyed mathematics but was inclined to be lazy in his study habits. He would read a lesson through just once, then depend on remembering enough of it to get by. Time that might have been used more profitably with his textbooks he spent reading novels, but when June arrived, he stood again in the middle in class ratings.

The summer of 1841 brought his long anticipated ten-week furlough and chance to return home to see his family. Grant did not return to Georgetown. While he had been away at school, Jesse had sold the retail business at Georgetown and moved the family to Bethel, Ohio, in adjoining Clermont County. Here he had opened a much larger tannery, devoted exclusively to wholesale business with retail outlets in Cincinnati and the booming lead-mining town of Galena, Illinois. Waiting to greet Grant were his younger brothers and sisters. Orvil, Simpson, Clara and Virginia, along with a new baby, Mary Frances, born since he left home. In anticipation of the homecoming, Jesse had bought him a handsome new colt. Grant would remember that summer as the happiest of his life. He passed the long, lazy days visiting with his family and relatives, breaking the new colt and making frequent trips to Georgetown to see old friends. Then all too soon it was time

Cadet Sam Grant

to return to West Point. As Grant boarded the river steamer to return, his mind was made up at last about his future. On graduation he hoped to apply for a position teaching mathematics at the academy. Once his four years service was completed, he would use this background to secure a professorship at some civilian university.

Grant found his junior year neither difficult nor particularly interesting. Most of the disinterest resulted from the fact that astronomy was the only course he had that year which was related to mathematics. Then the year was over and at last he was one of the elite first classmen, who gathered around the adjutant's bulletin board handing out nicknames to the new arrivals. There were 164 plebes in 1842, the largest class ever to enter West Point. The most promising was dapper, handsome George B. McClellan, son of a wealthy Philadelphia family and such a genius that the academy had waived its age requirement to admit him at only fifteen. The least promising was an awkward nineteen-year-old from the backwoods of Virginia, Thomas J. Jackson, who arrived dressed in homespun and carrying two sweat-stained saddlebags slung over his shoulders. It would be many years before "Old Jack," as he was dubbed, would win another nickname, "Stonewall," but there was something about his serious, quiet manner as well as the clumsy way he stumbled over the heels of the cadets ahead of him in drill, that reminded many cadets of "Uncle Sam" Grant in his own first year.

Grant's roommate for his last year was Frederick Dent, a handsome, soft-spoken youth from Missouri. As a first classman, Grant was elected president of the Dialectic, the campus literary society, and helped organize a secret society, the T.I.O. or Twelve In One. A bachelor organization devoted to good-fellowship, the members wore identical rings which they swore never to remove until the day when they married and the rings were given to their wives.

Grant's happiest hours were spent in the riding hall astride York, a huge bay horse that had been considered intractable until Grant had gentled him. As he worked out, he usually had an admiring audience of younger cadets. In addition to his prowess as a horseman, Grant had a reputation for imperturbable coolness in any situation. One day while waiting for the start of an engineering class, the cadets passed around and admired an enormous heirloom watch that belonged to one of the members. When the instructor strode into the class, Grant hastily slipped the watch out of sight inside his coat, planning to return it later. Called to the front to solve a problem, Grant had just written the solution on the board and was beginning his explanation when everyone was startled by a loud bonging noise. Annoyed, the instructor asked to have the door closed. The bonging grew louder. Grant guessed the truth. The watch, which chimed the hour, had purposely been set to go off during recitation. While the harassed professor bounded around the room searching everywhere for the offending noise, Grant calmly continued with his explanation as though nothing had happened until the watch ran down.

In June when the standings were posted, Grant was listed twenty-first among thirty-nine cadets who remained from the original class. The graduation exercises included an exhibition of horsemanship. As the riders completed their group maneuvers and formed a long line down the center of the hall, the ridingmaster strode forward and raised the jumping bar to a notch above his head. "Cadet Grant," he commanded. Mounted on York, Grant trotted out of line, made a half circle of the ring and galloped down the long line of cadets, taking the huge horse easily over the bar and setting an academy record for the high jump that would stand for twenty-five years.

In required quality of leadership, the army ranked its divisions into engineering, ordnance, artillery, dragoons and infantry. The graduates were allowed to make their choice of service in order of their class standing, with only the most brilliant permitted to choose the engineers. The next on the list could chose from ordnance on down, continuing in this manner to the lowest in the class, who had no choice but infantry. Grant's class was not an outstanding one. No graduate was allowed to choose engineering that year and only six went to ordnance. Grant's rank in the middle allowed only a choice between dragoons and infantry. He named the dragoons as his preference, though his orders would not arrive until he was home on the three-month leave granted after graduation.

The four years at West Point had changed Grant's appearance. He weighed exactly the same as he had on entering the academy, 117 pounds, but he was slender now, for he had grown six inches and outwardly he was much more poised and self-assured. But his determination not to become a professional soldier had not changed. A month after his return to Bethel, when his orders came through and he learned that there had been no openings in the dragoons and he was being assigned to the Fourth Infantry at Jefferson Barracks, Missouri, he was not disturbed. He considered it only a temporary assignment, for on leaving the academy he had been assured that he would be considered for a position teaching mathematics as soon as there was an opening.

Chapter III

Love and War

It was mid-August before Grant's new uniforms arrived. Dressed in his blue military coat, lighter blue trousers with a white stripe down the side, with his glistening new sword strapped at his side, he rode off to Cincinnati to show off his finery.

His conceit lasted as far as the city's outskirts where a ragged urchin ran along beside his horse to jeer, "Oh, ain't I the big Injun! Soldier, will you work? No, sirree . . . Oh, ain't he the big 'un."

Several days later a Bethel stableman, who fancied himself the town comic, appeared in a pair of ragged blue pants with a strip of white sheeting fastened down the side in strutting imitation of the young officer. Thoroughly mortified, Grant wore civilian clothes for the remainder of his leave. These two incidents left him, in his own words, "with a distaste for military uniform that I never recovered from."

Along with his fellow graduates, Grant had been assigned the rank of brevet second lieutenant, the brevet signifying that, while he was entitled to the command and pay of a second lieutenant, he was not yet listed on the army's permanent rolls. Due to the small size of the standing army, plus the fact that there was no provision for retirement of overage officers, advancement depended almost entirely on the death or resignation of officers farther up the line. As openings appeared, the new graduates would be admitted one by one to the permanent ranks.

On September 20, 1843, Grant reported to Jefferson Barracks, ten miles north of St. Louis and at that time the army's largest military post. The whitewashed limestone barracks which housed the officers and enlisted men formed three sides of a large central parade ground. Beyond these were other outbuildings, a brick hospital, stables, flower and vegetable gardens.

Sixteen companies of the Third and Fourth Infantry were stationed at Jefferson Barracks. Commanding the Fourth Infantry to which Grant was assigned was Colonel Josiah H. Vose, a gallant old soldier in his midseventies. Too feeble to conduct drill personally any longer, he delegated most of his duties to a younger officer. After being shown to his quarters, Grant was assigned a seat at the bachelor officers' mess presided over by Captain Robert Buchanan, an able but unpopular officer known as a stickler for regulations. Already stationed at Jefferson Barracks were a number of young officers Grant had known at West Point, among them Second Lieutenant James Longstreet who soon became Grant's closest friend.

Life at the post was relatively easy. As long as the officers performed their minimal duties and reported for drill practice, their spare hours were their own. For most of the bachelor officers this meant visiting the taverns and gambling houses in St. Louis. The city held little attraction for Grant. He had never distinguished himself for studiousness at West Point, but now, in anticipation of the promised post as a mathematics instructor, he spent most of his spare time boning up on geometry, trigonometry and algebra.

Fred Dent, Grant's roommate during his senior year, had

been assigned to the Sixth Infantry farther west in Indian territory, but he had asked Grant to call on his parents who lived near St. Louis. Grant had been at Jefferson Barracks several weeks before he finally set out to make this duty call.

The Dent home, called White Haven, was located five miles away on the Gravois Road. The two-story white house with slender columns supporting the long front veranda was typically Southern in appearance. Behind it were the usual outbuildings, barns and slave quarters. Here Grant met Colonel Frederick Dent, a white-haired, crusty gentleman in his midsixties, Mrs. Dent and Ellen, Emily and Louis, the three younger children who were living at home. An older boy, George, was married, while the oldest daughter, Julia, had just completed finishing school and was spending the winter with relatives. According to talkative, six-year-old Emmy, Julia was the most beautiful girl in Missouri as well as their father's favorite. Mr. Dent had never served in the army, but bore the title of colonel out of respect. A lifelong Democrat, he was inclined to grow choleric when arguing politics. To Mrs. Dent's amusement, Grant with his quiet, unruffled manner was one of the few men able to argue with the colonel without throwing him into a tantrum.

Soon Grant became a frequent visitor at White Haven, often riding over in the company of Longstreet to accept Mrs. Dent's invitations to dinner. In early February, Julia returned home. Of medium height, with a gracefully rounded figure and dark brown hair and eyes that set off a pale, almost luminous complexion, she was every bit as pretty as Emmy had described. Best of all, she was a superb horsewoman. Grant's visits became even more frequent. He and Julia slipped away from the family to take long rides together and she became his constant companion at all the post's dances.

Grant's increasing visits to White Haven brought about his first run-in with Captain Buchanan, head of the bachelors' mess. Buchanan had imposed an arbitrary rule that any officer who was late to the table would be fined a bottle of wine. One evening as Grant was slipping into his seat a few minutes after the others, Buchanan looked up angrily. "Grant, you're late again; that will be another bottle of wine, sir."

Grant tried to pass off the criticism lightly. "That makes three bottles of wine in ten days, sir. If I am fined again, I may have to repudiate."

Buchanan's face flushed. "Young people should be seen, not heard, sir!" He silenced the young lieutenant as though he were a schoolboy.

A short time later Grant had a more serious encounter with Buchanan. In the absence of his captain, Grant was drilling their company on the parade grounds. Noting the small number of men taking part, Buchanan ordered the drill halted. "Where are the rest of your men?" he demanded angrily as though Grant was personally accountable.

"Absent on leave at your orders, sir." Grant replied.

"You're lying," Buchanan snapped.

Though noted for his cool temper, Grant was sensitive to any reflection on his honor. Ordering a sergeant to return the company to barracks, Grant drew his sword, put the tip to Buchanan's chest and demanded an apology. Buchanan apologized, but after that they treated each other with an icy civility that barely concealed the enmity between them.

Grant's differences with Buchanan seemed minor compared to a new concern that swept Jefferson Barracks that spring. Back at West Point, the cadets had been forbidden to discuss politics. Now that there was no restriction, everyone was worriedly discussing the Texas problem.

Originally a frontier province belonging to Mexico, Texas had been settled in the 1820s by United States citizens, most of them from the Southern, slave-owning states. In return for their land grants, these settlers were supposed to become Mexican citizens, but they retained their ties with the United States, refusing to trade with Mexico City or obey Mexican laws which abolished slavery. In 1836, while Grant was still a schoolboy in Georgetown, the Texans had defeated the army of General Santa Anna, broken away from Mexico and set up an independent republic. Four years later when Texas asked for admission to the Union, it set off a heated debate in Congress. Since Mexico had never recognized the new republic, in Mexican eyes the annexation would appear as an unlawful seizure of their territory and could lead to war. Some abolitionists carried the argument farther, claiming it was all a Southern scheme to add more slave territory to the Union.

Grant was not so naïve as to believe that the annexation of Texas was a slave-owners' plot. Along with many of his fellow officers he saw it as the first step in a new and potentially dangerous philosophy that was sweeping the nation. In a few years this philosophy would be dignified with the name "Manifest Destiny." Since the Louisiana Purchase in 1803, the United States had been rapidly expanding westward. All over the country, there was a growing sentiment that it was America's rightful destiny that this expansion should not be stopped until it reached the Pacific Coast, including not only California, which also belonged to Mexico, but the Oregon Territory, which was jointly owned by the United States and Great Britain.

So far a coalition between the abolitionists and those who hoped to prevent war had successfully blocked the annexation of Texas. But in April 1844, as President John Tyler prepared to present the issue to Congress again, the Third Infantry was ordered out of Jefferson Barracks to Fort Jessup in Louisiana near the Texas border.

Reasoning that the Fourth Infantry might soon follow, Grant applied for a twenty-day leave beginning May 1, to return home to Bethel. His reasoning was correct; only a few days after he reached Ohio, he received a letter from a fellow officer telling him that the Fourth Infantry was leaving for Louisiana on May 7. Instead of enjoying the brief respite, Grant was suddenly restless. He was in love with Julia Dent. If he waited to rejoin the rest of his regiment in Louisiana, he might never see her again.

Aboard the next boat, Grant rushed back to Jefferson Barracks. The Fourth had already left, but he asked for and was granted permission to use his remaining days of leave to take care of "some important business." Then, without stopping at the barracks, he mounted his horse and set off for White Haven. It had been raining for several days and normally placid Gravois Creek was flooded. Grant rode a short distance along the bank and plunged in. Horse and rider were immediately swept downstream but finaly managed to make it to the other side. Grant galloped on to White Haven, arriving so caked with mud and bedraggled looking that the entire Dent family burst into laughter.

For several days Grant could not work up his courage to propose to Julia. Then one morning, when the young people were to attend a wedding, he persuaded her brother to take his horse while he drove Julia alone in the buggy. When they reached the creek, it was still flooded and Julia wanted to turn back. Grant tried to persuade her that it was safe to cross. Finally she gave in, warning him that she was entrusting him with her life. It was the opening Grant needed. Once safely on the other side, he used the incident to ask her to entrust her life to him forever. By the time they joined the others, Julia had promised to marry him.

Back at White Haven, Grant did not find such a convenient opening for speaking to Colonel Dent. Though he had been welcome at White Haven as a guest, Grant knew that the colonel did not approve of either a Yankee or a soldier as a prospective son-in-law. Jessie Benton, the daughter of the colonel's closest friend, Senator Thomas Hart Benton, had married an army captain, John C. Frémont. According to Colonel Dent, when Frémont immediately set off on a series of long exploring expeditions to the West, he had abandoned his wife to a life of loneliness and neglect, a fate Dent did not wish for any of his daughters. When Grant left White Haven to rejoin his regiment, the engagement remained a secret.

It was June 3, 1844, when Grant reached Camp Salubrity, near Natchitoches, Louisiana. Located on a sandy, forested bluff overlooking the Sabine River, the camp had been thrown hastily together to accommodate the overflow from Fort Jessup twenty miles to the west. Instead of limestone barracks, the men lived in tents now, but Grant enjoyed the outdoor life. There was not a great deal to do. He wrote long letters to Julia, which she answered promptly, and one letter to her father asking for her hand in marriage, to which he received no reply. Friends had packed his belongings for the move to Camp Salubrity, but along the way most of his mathematics books had been lost. Grant did not bother to replace them. As the prospect of war drew closer, his hopes for the teaching appointment faded.

At Camp Salubrity, Grant met recently breveted Brigadier General Zachary Taylor, who was to be their leader. Next to General Winfield Scott, Taylor was considered the most able officer in the army. The difference between "Old Rough and Ready" Taylor and "Old Fuss and Feathers" Scott was extreme. Taylor had not attended West Point but had risen from the ranks and was noted for his casualness of dress. As he reviewed the troops, a wad of chewing tobacco in his mouth, dressed in a long, stained linen duster and battered straw hat, and sitting sidewise on his favorite horse, Old Whitey, with one leg hooked casually around the pommel, he looked more like a backwoods farmer than a general. But the men who had served under him claimed he could fight circles around any other general, even Scott himself.

Love and War

There was no fighting that summer, fall or winter. For the soldiers at Camp Salubrity it was a time of waiting while politicians fought the political battles of an election year. The candidate of the Democratic Party was James K. Polk, who made the admission of Texas and the acquisition of most of the Oregon Territory the major planks of his campaign platform. Opposing him was Henry Clay, the Whig candidate. When the abolitionist Whigs broke away to form their own separate Liberty Party, Polk won the election handily. By March 1, 1845, Polk had carried through his first campaign promise and Congress had approved the annexation of Texas, requiring only the ratification of the other states.

Applying for another leave, Grant took off for St. Louis and White Haven. He arrived as Colonel Dent was getting ready to leave on a trip to Washington, D.C. Seeing it was impossible to delay any longer, he blurted out his request for permission to marry Julia. The colonel was caught off guard. With war fever in the air his opinion about military men had softened, and there were the added pleas of Julia and her mother. Somewhat begrudgingly, he gave his consent. Grant had hoped to be married during his leave, but with Colonel Dent away in Washington this became an impossibility. When it was time to return to Camp Salubrity, he had to be content with the knowledge that Julia would be waiting for him.

In early July, with the ratification of the admission of Texas completed, the Third and Fourth Infantry moved south to New Orleans. New recruits arrived daily. The imminence of war was weeding out many older officers who were no longer physically fit for active duty. Grant's commander, Colonel Vose, refused to resign and seek a safer position in civilian life. He forced himself out onto the parade ground to take command, barked a few orders and fell dead. Moved up to replace him was hard-drinking, sixty-five-year-old Colonel William Whistler.

By the end of the month General Taylor, with part of the

Third Regiment, had set sail for Corpus Christi, Texas. A week later, Grant and his company followed aboard the sailing vessel *Suviah*. It was Grant's first sea voyage. By the time they hove to in the shallow waters where the Nueces River emptied into the Gulf of Mexico, Grant was confident enough of his accomplishments as a sailor to try to go over the side unassisted by the ropes which lowered the supplies to smaller boats below. To his chagrin he immediately was flipped head over heels and suspended upside down by one leg, then plunged into the water below. He was a good swimmer. All that was injured was his pride as the laughing sailors hauled him back to deck, astride a large wooden bucket lowered on the end of a rope.

Until the arrival of the troops, Corpus Christi had been a ramshackle settlement of about 150 persons, most of whom made their living by smuggling. Extending back from the coast were miles of rolling prairie blanketed with waving green grass as high as a man's waist, with here and there a glimpse of the blue waters of the Nueces River as it wound inland. Green turtles and oysters were plentiful at the river's mouth and the prairies abounded with duck, wild turkey and deer. Grant did not care for hunting, but the grasslands were also the home of great herds of wild horses, many of which were rounded up and driven into camp for army use. Grant purchased one beautiful stallion, so wild and intractable that no other officer would bid on it. A sizable crowd gathered to watch him ride the horse for the first time. Grant ordered the animal blindfolded until he was in the saddle. When the blindfold was whipped off, the stallion began to buck and whirl in a vain attempt to throw his rider. At the first sign the animal was weakening, Grant gave the stallion its head and dug in his spurs. Horse and rider took off like a cannonball, thundering through the camp and out of sight onto the prairie. At the end of three hours, Longstreet was about to organize a search party when he heard shouts. It was Grant, trotting calmly back past the long lines of tents. Both man and horse were drenched with sweat.

By October additional regiments of infantry, artillery and dragoons had increased the camp to four thousand men. Among the new arrivals were many of Grant's former classmates at West Point, including his future brother-in-law, Fred Dent. Occasionally Grant escorted the wagon trains traveling 150 miles to San Antonio, the nearest town of any size; but most of their supplies arrived by sea, though the shallow waters hampered the landing operations. One day when some soldiers failed to understand their orders for dredging one of the channels, Grant leaped into the water fully clothed to demonstrate how the work should be done, to the amusement of his more fastidious comrades. The incident brought him to the attention of "Old Rough and Ready," who was attracted by the laughter. "I wish I had more officers like Grant," he observed to an aide.

In December 1845, Grant received notice from the War Department that he had been promoted from brevet to full second lieutenant. Of the thirty-nine men in his graduating class, only ten others had received this advancement, five previously and another five at the same time as his promotion.

President Polk had sent John Slidell as ambassador to Mexico in hopes of peacefully settling the Texas dispute. He failed to reach an agreement with Mexico's President José Herrera. When Herrera's government was overthrown, the new president, General Mariano Paredes, proved even more adamant and ordered Slidell to leave the country. With Mexico refusing either to negotiate or to make an open declaration of war, the United States found itself in an embarrassing position. Because of possible adverse world opinion, Polk did not want to initiate hostilities. Somehow Mexico must be goaded into making the first move. Mexico claimed that the Texas boundary was the

Nueces River; the Texans claimed that it was the Rio Grande River 150 miles farther south. Early in 1846, General Taylor received orders to march south as soon as weather permitted and build a fort on the banks of the Rio Grande opposite the Mexican city of Matamoros.

Those next weeks, while they waited for the end of the rainy season, Grant struggled with his conscience. He was opposed to all wars and particularly opposed to this war, which he felt was being instigated by the United States in order to seize Mexican territory. Deep in his heart he wanted to resign, but he had accepted a free education from the government and sworn to serve it. In the end, he decided that his first debt was to his country. The decision was not one of which he would ever be proud. Years later in his *Memoirs* he described the Mexican War "as one of the most unjust [wars] ever waged by a stronger nation against a weaker."

By March 8, the rains had abated and General Taylor set out with 2500 men across the Nueces River into the disputed territory. Grant's company was in the last column. The country was flat, the water sparse and the heat so intense that miles inland the marching men could see mirages of the blue Gulf waters and ships riding at anchor reflected overhead in the burning sky. At one river crossing they heard the sound of bugles and a wave of excitement raced through the lines, but it turned out to be only a small Mexican scouting party that galloped off as they approached. By March 28, they had reached the Rio Grande and could see the gleaming white walls and red tile roofs of Matamoros across the river, with hundreds of citizens crowded onto the rooftops to watch their arrival.

The following morning they saw that new breastworks had been built around the city and a Mexican general sent a message across the river ordering them to withdraw. For the two months they remained across the river building the fort, there was no attack on the workers themselves, but there were several skirmishes between scouting parties sent out by both sides. When one scouting party of dragoons fell into a Mexican trap, with sixteen killed and forty-seven captured, Taylor wrote to Washington that they might consider that hostilities had begun.

By the first of May their supplies were running low. Leaving five hundred men to man the new fort and taking the other two thousand, including Grant's company, Taylor started down the Rio Grande to Point Isabel, twenty-five miles away at the mouth of the river, where American ships had already set up a new base of supplies.

For two days they were kept busy at Point Isabel, unloading supplies and men. Then one morning Grant awakened to what he thought was the distant rumble of one of the frequent thunderstorms. But Taylor and the more experienced veterans recognized it immediately as distant cannon fire. The fort up the river was under seige; the war had begun. To the amazement of Grant and many of the younger officers, Taylor did not rush off immediately to the aid of the fort but continued with his primary concern of unloading their supplies. It was May 7 before Taylor finally started the march inland with around three thousand men.

The country was flat, covered with tall, stiff grass as high as a man's waist with a distant rim of green trees marking the banks of the river. As they continued the march on the morning of May 8 without any sign of the enemy, Grant tried to reassure himself that it was all some kind of dream and the Mexicans would not be so foolish as to fight. But shortly after midday, as they approached an area where the woods extended inland, word went back along the lines that the enemy had been spotted. Six thousand strong, the Mexicans were drawn up in front of the trees in battle formation. Soon Grant could see their blue uniforms and tall shako caps, and the sunlight reflecting from their brass cannon and the long spears of the cavalrymen.

Just out of range of the enemy cannon, Taylor ordered a halt. Sitting lazily astride Old Whitey, he studied the opposing lines, then ordered his own troops rearranged in battle formation with the light artillery and their two heavy cannon placed at intervals along the line of infantrymen. After that, a half dozen men from each company were instructed to carry their companions' canteens to the river and fill them. When each soldier had taken a long drink of water, Taylor ordered the march resumed.

Only a few of the American soldiers carried the new percussion-cap musket. The majority, like Grant, were armed with old-fashioned flintlocks which had an effective range of less than one hundred yards. As it turned out this made little difference. The battle of Palo Alto (tall tree) was to be principally an artillery duel.

As soon as the march was renewed, the Mexicans opened fire, though their guns were still out of range. As the Americans moved closer, cannonballs began glancing off the ground ahead and bending long trails in the grass so that the men could see them coming and dodge them. Once within their own range, Taylor ordered the artillery to the front and opened up a return fire. Grant could see the first shots take effect, cutting swaths through the enemy ranks. The din of the barrage mounted. The Mexicans tried several cavalry charges, which were repelled. At one point the dry grass ignited, sending up such billows of black smoke that all firing had to be stopped temporarily until the fire burned out. Grant never got close enough to use his flintlock, but a soldier near him was killed by a cannonball which sped on to rip off the lower jaw of a fellow officer. The Mexicans had the advantage in number of cannons, but they fired only solid shot, while the American artillery spewed canister, which was more deadly. The battle ended at dusk with the Mexicans in retreat. The Americans counted a minimal loss of nine dead and fifty wounded.

The following day, March 9, as the march continued, they found the enemy waiting again at Resaca de la Palma, where a number of small ponds had formed in an old river channel and the terrain was covered with heavy underbrush. Having witnessed the power of the American artillery, the Mexican commanders had chosen to make this stand from cover where the cannon were less effective. The infantry was sent forward in small units to fight through the tangled growth in what Grant described as a "pellmell affair with everybody for himself." Grant led some of his men into the brush, crawling on his stomach and returning the enemy fire. In a small clearing they jubilantly surrounded a Mexican colonel and a number of soldiers, only to find when they escorted them back behind their own lines that the group had been captured earlier by another unit. Grant wrote with wry humor of the incident: "My exploit was equal to that of the soldier who boasted he had cut off the leg of one of the enemy. When asked why he had not cut off his head, he replied, 'Someone had done that before.'"

The battle ended in a rout of the enemy, many of the fleeing Mexicans leaping into the Rio Grande where almost as many were drowned as had been killed on the battlefield. Again the American losses were light, with twenty-nine killed and eighty-two wounded, while the Mexicans lost close to a thousand. In the two days of fighting Grant had not displayed any great heroism, but he had made a comforting discovery. Though there had been a nervous churning in his stomach as they started away from Point Isabel, once under fire all nervousness had left him.

Pushing on to the fort they found that it had withstood the seige with only two casualties, one of them the commander, Major Jacob Brown. Originally dubbed Fort Texas, it was renamed Fort Brown in his honor and today is the site of Brownsville, Texas. Ten days later they crossed the river and occupied Matamoros without resistance. The Mexican forces had withdrawn into the interior.

For two months the troops remained in Matamoros, receiving supplies and new recruits. Many of the volunteers had signed for only one year, a term so short that it was hardly worth training them. The greatest number came from the Southern states, where tempers ran hot to kill "some greasers" and "avenge the Alamo." Untrained, undisciplined and rowdy, they filled the streets with their carousing. Their officers were even more of a problem since the majority were political appointees with no military experience. One newly appointed general arrived in a fancy buggy which he planned to drive all the way to Mexico City. Many Southerners, accustomed to having slaves wait on them, expected the regular army soldiers to fetch and carry. Even the usually placid Grant received a jolt when a volunteer company arrived from Georgetown, led by an untrained youth who outranked Grant as a captain. Another surprising political appointee was former Ohio Congressman Thomas Hamer, who had secured Grant's appointment to West Point. Though Hamer bore the rank of brigadier general, he was intelligent enough to know his own weaknesses. He immediately sought out Grant. The two rode out into the country where, seated on a small hummock and employing sticks and stones as military units, Grant attempted to give his former benefactor lessons in basic strategy. In one of his letters home, Hamer described Grant as "a most remarkable and valuable young soldier," adding, "Of course, Lieutenant Grant is too young for command."

Throughout it all, Grant marveled at the patience and equanimity "Old Rough and Ready" showed in handling the new volunteers. Back in the States, President Polk had managed to settle the Oregon boundary question peacefully with Great Britain. On June 15, 1846, when a treaty was signed extending the boundary between the United States and Canada westward along the forty-ninth parallel, the threat of a third war with Great Britain vanished. Encouraged by glowing newspaper accounts of the battles of Palo Alto and Resaca de la Palma to believe the war in Mexico was almost over, volunteers anxious to be in on the final victory flooded the recruiting centers. Aware that he could neither supply nor train so many undisciplined men, Taylor began discharging many of the one-year men. From his scouts he had learned that the Mexicans were massing their strength at Monterrey, 170 miles to the southwest. Since the Mexicans would not come to the Americans, the Americans would have to march to them. For the regular army men who would carry the brunt of the fighting, the war had only begun.

Chapter IV

On to Mexico City

By the end of July, the American troops were ready to leave Matamoros. The first stage of the journey up the Rio Grande to the town of Camargo was relatively easy, since the river was navigable to that point and supplies could be transported by boat. From there the army faced a 150-mile march across rugged, sparsely inhabited country to Monterrey. What wagons were available would be required by the artillery. To carry the food, tents and equipment for his six thousand men, General Taylor would rely on pack mules and hired native drivers.

To ease the burden of his already overtaxed Quartermaster Corps, Taylor asked each regimental commander to appoint his own quartermaster, who would assume the responsibility of handling animals and supplies for their regiments. By now elderly Colonel Whistler of the Fourth Infantry had been replaced by a younger commander, Lieutenant Colonel John Garland. When Garland looked over his list of officers, Second Lieutenant U. S. Grant, with his proved ability in handling animals and family background in the draying business, seemed the ideal choice.

Grant did not agree. "I respectfully protest against being assigned to a duty which removes me from sharing in the dangers and honors of service with my company at the front and respectfully ask to be permitted to resume my place in line," he wrote. Garland read the protest and informed Grant that it had been denied. There was nothing further Grant could do. When the army started for Monterrey on September 5, he found himself with the inglorious job of being "general housekeeper" for his regiment.

While his fellow officers rode ahead, Grant and his supply train trailed in the choking dust at the rear. Each morning, after supervising the loading of the animals, Grant was the last to leave camp. Once on the road he faced the task of curbing runaways, repacking loosened loads, shifting supplies as animals gave out and somehow managing to catch up with his regiment before dusk in order to make camp. Each evening brought the additional work of providing forage for the mules, examining animals for saddle sores or illness, securing replacements for those that had given out, mending harnesses, replacing uniforms and lost equipment, and supplying the camp with firewood.

Somehow Grant managed the task without too much difficulty. From his position in the dusty tail of the column, he even found time to enjoy the scenery and speculate about the inhabitants. He liked what he had seen of Mexico and its people. He pitied the lower-class Mexicans for their poverty but admired their warm family life, the gay little gardens that surrounded even the shabbiest hovels and their ability to find happiness under conditions that would have been unendurable to most North Americans. He particularly respected the endurance of the Mexican foot soldiers, most of whom had been conscripted against their will and thought nothing of marching twenty-five and on occasion fifty miles a day, while the average march for the United States troops was fifteen miles.

Aside from his initial protest to Garland, he did not complain of his duties. Only his long letters to Julia revealed his inner restlessness. "Aren't you getting tired of hearing of war, war, war? ... Here it is five months that we have been at war and as yet but two battles. I do wish this would close. If we have to fight, I would like to do it all at once and then make friends," he wrote.

On September 19, the army set up camp at Walnut Springs, two miles north of Monterrey. In the distance Grant could see the whitewashed buildings and tile roofs of the town nestled against a backdrop of sunburned mountains. During the time Taylor had been delayed at Matamoros, Mexican General Pedro de Ampudia had been fortifying the town and bringing up reinforcements so that he was reported to have more than ten thousand men under arms. To the south the city was protected by a river. To the east were two forts, Tenaria and Diablo, to the west hill entrenchments topped by a strong fortress called the Bishop's Palace, while to the north, standing well out onto the plain between the city and the American camp, was a massive emplacement, the Black Fort. Should the Americans get past these outer defenses, inside the city almost every roof had been sandbagged, every house fortified. In the very center of the city was another huge fortification, the Citadel, which equaled the Black Fort in size.

After studying the situation, Taylor ordered General William J. Worth to lead the main attack from the west by way of the Bishop's Palace, while other units assisted him with diversionary action on the east and north.

The following night Worth moved his men into position and on the morning of September 21, the battle began. As Grant went about his chores back at Walnut Springs, he could hear the distant rumble of the opening fire. With his pack animals secured, curiosity overcame him. Mounting a gray mare named Nellie, he rode out to see what was happening to his company. He found them in a small swale directly in front of the Black Fort. Moments after he arrived, Garland gave the order to charge. There seemed nothing for Grant to do but to charge with them. Within seconds, devastating fire from the Black Fort had mowed down one third of the men. Instead of retreating to the swale, Garland directed the survivors to the east where they immediately were caught in the crossfire from Fort Tenaria and another fortified building, the Tannery. With others of his company Grant reached the temporary protection of another swale. Tumbling down the slopes behind him came Garland's adjutant, Lieutenant Charles Hoskins, who had left his sickbed to go into action and already was so exhausted that he could barely stand. Dismounting, Grant gave Hoskins his horse. On foot, he had no choice but to remain with his company.

The fighting continued through the afternoon with brigades of volunteers rushed up to assist the battered Fourth Infantry. By nightfall the Tannery had been taken. One of the afternoon's casualties had been Lieutenant Hoskins. Grant ventured out after dark to ready his corpse for removal to the rear and retrieve Nellie. Back with the others, he was assigned to replace Hoskins as adjutant temporarily.

The next day they moved into the city, fighting from street to street and encountering deadly crossfire at each intersection. By now Worth's men had taken the Bishop's Palace and were moving in from the west. The following day Garland's men surged ahead of their support and had almost reached the central plaza when they discovered that they were running low on ammunition. Grant volunteered to ride for help. As he raced through the streets, he hooked a knee around the pommel and dropped Indian fashion below Nellie's shoulder at each intersection. Horse and rider shot by the cross streets so swiftly that no marksman was able to get them in his sights.

Unfortunately the ride was in vain. Before reinforcements could be rushed in, Garland was forced to pull back. By now Worth was moving steadily into the city. Instead of subjecting his men to the open fire of the streets, he moved from house to house, tunneling his way through the walls, so that his men were protected much of the time. On September 24, General Ampudia surrendered and the battle was over. Taylor gave the Mexican general generous terms, allowing him and most of his men to leave the city. The American casualties were 448 dead or wounded, the Mexican losses close to two thousand.

At Monterrey the troops settled down to another long wait while a new battle of politics raged back home. General Winfield Scott, commander in chief of the army, had been advising the opening of a second front by shipping troops to Veracruz to march directly inland against Mexico City. Scott was a Whig and known to be ambitious, which had influenced President Polk's decision to let Taylor direct the opening phase of the war. Though Taylor was also a Whig, he had never shown any signs of political ambition. Now, as a result of his victories, Taylor had become a hero back in the States and his name was already being suggested as the Whig candidate in the next Presidential election. In vain Polk tried to locate a Democrat general with the necessary experience to head the new expedition. When none could be found, he ordered Scott to Veracruz, hoping that he and Taylor would at least divide the honors and split the Whigs.

Some of Taylor's troops, including the Fourth Infantry, were ordered back to the Rio Grande to join Scott. It was January of 1847 before they got underway. Grant would have preferred to remain with Taylor, but at least the dreary months of waiting were over. During the three months at Monterrey as many soldiers had died of dysentery and tropical fevers as had been lost in battle, among them Grant's former benefactor, Brigadier General Tom Hamer.

From Camargo the Fourth continued downstream to the site of the old battlefield at Palo Alto, where a temporary camp had been established, until vessels could be secured to carry the men south to Veracruz. The one-year volunteers were being discharged, but others were arriving to take their places, along with units of the regular army being moved in from variout western outposts. At Palo Alto Grant met Captain Robert E. Lee, the brilliant young engineer who had graduated from West Point with an unblemished record and was reputed to be General Scott's special protégé.

At last the ships appeared and on March 6, Grant reached Antón Lizardo Bay, where Scott was assembling his forces. On March 9 they landed without opposition three miles south of Veracruz and began the bombardment of the city. When the army artillery proved ineffective, Scott brought ashore some heavy naval guns and by the end of the month the port city had been occupied.

The United States government was not the only one involved in political struggles. By now there had been an upheaval in the Mexican government and General Antonio Santa Anna, who had led the Mexican army in its unsuccessful battles against the Texans, had been called back from exile to head a new government. A wily and unscrupulous politician, Santa Anna persuaded the United States to allow him to pass through the American naval blockade on the promise that once he took over the government he would sue for peace. Instead, on arriving in Mexico City and finding the sentiment of the people was to continue fighting, Santa Anna assembled an army and marched north hoping to defeat Taylor's reduced forces. In a fierce two-day battle at Buena Vista in mid-February, the Mexican army was defeated again. Rushing back to Mexico City ahead of his straggling troops, Santa Anna displayed several regimental flags taken early in the battle and conned the people into believing he had won the victory. Now, with a newly organized army, he was reported to be marching east somewhere along the 260-mile-long road to Veracruz.

With summer and the deadly yellow-fever season approaching, Scott could not afford to keep his army in the tropical lowlands around Veracruz. In mid-April, he started inland with around eight thousand men along the winding road that climbed rapidly into the more healthful climate of the mountainous interior. The various divisions were spread out along the narrow road, with Grant and the Fourth Infantry well toward the rear.

Fifty miles up the road at a narrow defile called Cerro Gordo, where precipitous cliffs formed a natural defense, Santa Anna was waiting. From the sound of cannon fire ahead, then the sight of the wounded being shuttled back down the line, Grant learned that Santa Anna had successfully repelled their advance division. Scott immediately rushed forward his corps of engineers, which included Captain Lee and young Lieutenant George B. McClellan, who had entered West Point as the outstanding member of the plebe class during Grant's final year. Lee became the hero of the hour when he and the others devised a way to get the American cannon onto the heights above the enemy. In the battle that followed, the enemy was routed and Santa Anna was forced to flee on horseback, leaving behind his ornate carriage with his wooden peg leg inside. Soon unscrupulous peddlers back in the States would be selling hundreds of wooden legs to a gullible public, all reputedly the leg of old "Santa Anner."

For Grant, struggling up from the rear with his pack train, there was neither glory nor time for celebration. As mule after mule collapsed with exhaustion, loads had to be shifted to other animals. Men also collapsed from the heat and altitude. At first, Grant made room for them in the wagons. When there was no more room, he gave them water and stretched them out beside the road to be picked up by the surgeons. When he finally made camp at Cerro Gordo, there were animals to be unpacked and fed, food and tents to be distributed. Everywhere around him was the ugliness of the battle. Three thousand

Mexican soldiers had been taken prisoner and another twelve hundred had been slain, most of their shattered bodies still lying where they had fallen. Grant noticed that many of the dead were little more than boys. With his companions he watched a woman moving silently among the bodies, turning over each corpse. Kneeling beside one, she raised it into an old chair which she then strapped to her back and started away. Questioned by one of the men who knew a little Spanish, she replied that she had come seeking her "only child" to take him home for decent burial. Even if he had been able to carry a tune, Grant would not have felt like singing.

From Cerro Gordo they continued inland and on May 15 reached Puebla, a major city of eighty thousand located midway between the coast and the capital. Finding it undefended, they marched in with bands playing. Once dispersed, a few of the more exuberant soldiers took off in search of taverns and señoritas. Others, exhausted from the long march, lay down in the streets and went to sleep. As always, Grant was occupied unloading his mules and hunting forage.

At Puebla, Scott called a halt to wait for their supplies to catch up with them. When the pack trains were slow in arriving, Grant made forays into the countryside, rounding up beef and provisions for his regiment.

President Polk had sent peace envoys along with the army in hope of arranging terms with Santa Anna. As the weeks dragged by at Puebla with more troops falling ill from tropical fevers, it became evident that Santa Anna had no intentions of talking peace. While the Americans waited at Puebla, struggling to maintain themselves over their long supply lines and with their ranks being thinned by illness, the canny Mexican was building up his army and fortifying Mexico City for a final stand.

Early in August, breaking one of the cardinal rules of warfare by cutting off his supply lines, Scott called in the guards from along the supply route, left a token force to protect the sick at Puebla and ordered every able-bodied man on to Mexico City. If their supplies ran out, they were instructed to live off the land.

Once again the road climbed through the mountains, even higher now with snow-capped peaks rising to seventeen thousand feet. Finally they came through a high pass and saw their destination below: a great valley forty miles wide, dotted with blue lakes, cultivated squares of farmlands, the white buildings of small rural settlements and, far in the distance, the imposing walls and towering church steeples of the capital.

Because of the many lakes, almost all of the roads into the city lay along broad causeways which were subject to the concentrated fire of the defenders. On August 19, the attack was opened at the fortified village of Contreras along the approach from the south. Once again Captain Lee was the hero when he mapped a route through the Pedregal, a wilderness of rock and twisted lava, permitting the Americans to make a successful flanking maneuver. By August 20, Contreras had fallen and the troops had pushed on to take a heavily fortified convent at Churubusco. In two days of fighting, the American casualties were close to a thousand dead and wounded, almost one eighth of their total fighting force. An armistice was arranged and the peace envoys tried to deal with Santa Anna again. At the end of two weeks, when no agreement was reached, the fighting resumed.

Dominating Mexico City from a hill on the western perimeter was the great fortress of Chapultepec. Once the summer residence of the Spanish governors, it was now Mexico's National military academy and equivalent of West Point. Guarding the base of the hill were heavy entrenchments which ended on the south at the thick walls of an old mill, El Molino del Rey. Since the cannons on the heights of Chapultepec could cover the city below, the fortress became the prime target of the advance. On September 8, an attack was launched against El Molino del Rey. As a fusillade from the mill mowed down the first wave of soldiers, Grant went in with the second. Around him men were falling and animals screaming in pain as they went down in their harness. One of those hit was Julia's brother, Fred Dent. Grant could do nothing to help as he raced by in the charge of his own company.

Some of the Mexicans were withdrawing, but as Grant burst around a corner of a building, he saw a group still manning a gun on the mill roof. Seizing a nearby cart, he upended it so that the long traces could be used as a makeshift scaling ladder to reach the roof and capture the gun crew. Later, he made light of the exploit by comparing it to the capture of the colonel and his soldiers at Resaca de la Palma. As he reached the roof, he saw soldiers from another company already coming up from the other side.

With the Mexicans withdrawing toward Chapultepec, Grant was able to run back to where Fred had fallen, make certain that his wounds were not fatal and lay him out on top of a flat wall where he could easily be found by the surgeons.

For two days they camped near the mill, resting and caring for the wounded; then Scott ordered up the heavy artillery for a new assault. While other companies were engaged in taking Chapultepec, Grant was in one of the first units that advanced into the city, using the archways of a stone aqueduct that paralleled the road for protection. When the aqueduct suddenly veered, they were stopped by a street barricade. Grant managed to get some of his men across the road to the shelter of a wall. Using this as cover, they slipped around behind the barricade and knocked out the guns.

Fighting from street to street, they pushed on into the city, sleeping that night in the houses they had overrun. By now the division led by General Worth had been diverted around to the north to the San Cosme gate, but heavy gunfire from the roofs of the surrounding buildings blocked their entrance. Commandeering a howitzer from a passing artillery unit, Grant dragged the dismantled gun to the tall belfry of a nearby church, reassembled it and directed the fire onto the roofs below it to help clear the gate. The following day word came that Santa Anna was fleeing the city. On September 15 the Americans pushed on to the central plaza where they raised the Stars and Stripes.

As far as the fighting was concerned, the war was over, but it was to be another six months before the peace terms would be formally settled. While Taylor and Scott had been fighting in Mexico, other American forces had successfully seized California. As reparations for the war, the United States was asking not only California and Texas, but Mexico's claims to all of the country between them: what is today Arizona, New Mexico, Nevada, Colorado and the southern portion of Wyoming.

While the wounded were moved to the coast for return to the States, the rest of the troops settled down in Mexico as occupation forces. Stationed at Tacubaya on the outskirts of Mexico City, Grant resumed his quartermaster duties. Except for his eagerness to rejoin Julia, he did not find his duties too unpleasant. He joined the Aztec Society, an honorary society composed of the surviving officers of the war. From time to time he was granted leaves, which he used to travel and see the sights of Mexico. For his gallantry in action at El Molino del Rey, he was given a brevet promotion to first lieutenant, and for the action at the San Cosme belfry, another brevet promotion to captain. More satisfying in Grant's estimation, however, was the notification that he had been promoted to first lieutenant on the army's permanent rolls. This would be the rank he would hold when he returned to the States.

Of the surviving members of Grant's West Point class, only eight others had received two brevets for gallantry, placing

Grant among the upper fourth of his class. But when the members of the Aztec Society discussed the officers whose conduct during the war had marked them for future leadership, Grant's name was never mentioned. Lee, who had been breveted all the way to colonel, was considered the most outstanding. Others, such as George B. McClellan, Don Carlos Buell, Joseph Johnston, Braxton Bragg, George H. Thomas and William Sherman, the latter serving in California, were selected the potential leaders of the future.

On March 10, 1848, the Treaty of Guadalupe Hidalgo formally ended the war. But it was June 12 before Grant left Mexico City with the last units of the army to return home to Julia after a separation of four years.

Chapter V

Between Wars

For a moment twelve-year-old Emmy Dent did not recognize the lean stranger who rode up to the veranda of White Haven in the summer of 1848. Then her excited shrieks brought Julia and the rest of the family. Grant had shaved off the red beard he had worn through the Mexican campaign. His once full face was thinner and deeply tanned, with the beginnings of crow's-feet around his eyes from hours of squinting into the hot Mexican sun.

There had been no change in Julia's feelings. The faithfulness with which she had waited for her fiancé these last four years had broken down Colonel Dent's reservations about the marriage. Leaving the Dents to make the wedding preparations, Grant continued north for a visit with his own family. Jesse Grant was noisily jubilant over the return of his son. No one scoffed at his bragging now; everyone in Bethel considered Grant a hero. Old friends commented on the change in the once diffident youth. No longer shy, Grant talked easily and amusingly of his experience in Mexico. He had brought a Mexican youth named Gregory home with him as his personal servant. Gregory immediately became the town favorite as he displayed his roping ability in the tannery yard, lassoing horses,

Between Wars

pigs, dogs and even small boys with equal ease. When it was time for Grant to return to Missouri, he left Gregory behind to learn the tanner's trade.

To provide a home for his younger children while they were in school, Colonel Dent had purchased a town house in St. Louis. A substantial brick house at the corner of Fourth and Cerre Streets, it was the scene of Grant's and Julia's wedding at eight o'clock in the evening of August 22. Captain James Longstreet was one of Grant's ushers.

For a honeymoon, Grant took Julia north to meet his family. If Colonel Dent had entertained reservations about his daughter marrying a Northerner, Jesse Grant, with his antislavery sentiments, had equal misgivings about a Southern daughter-in-law, particularly one who was reported to own slaves of her own. But Julia left her servants behind. Once in Bethel, her sunny disposition and graceful manners won Jesse's and Hannah's hearts. Those first months of marriage were so happy that Grant applied for an extension of leave.

It was November when he reported to his new post at Detroit. His old commander, General Zachary Taylor, had been elected to the Presidency only the week before. Compared to the assignments of many of his fellow officers, Grant had fared well. The following spring, as news of the big gold strike in California drew thousands of emigrants west, many of the younger officers were assigned to frontier outposts along the overland trail.

With the close of the war, Colonel Whistler had been restored to the command of the Fourth Infantry, but the office of regimental quartermaster was retained. Grant found the peacetime duties relatively easy. He and Julia rented a house on East Fort Street. Grant enjoyed drinking, playing cards and horse racing with his masculine friends. Though he did not care a great deal for dancing, he escorted Julia to all the post cotillions and with their close friends and neighbors, Captain and Mrs. John Gore, they entertained at frequent small parties for the other officers and their wives. In the spring of 1850, Julia returned to White Haven to await the birth of their first child, Frederick Dent Grant, who was born in May.

The following year, when the Fourth Infantry was transferred to Madison Barracks at Sacketts Harbor, New York, Grant took Julia and the baby with him. Again the Gores were their neighbors and life was much the same as before. It was not until the spring of 1852, with eight years of service drawing to a close, that Grant faced the important decision of whether or not to remain in the army. With the end of the war the army had dropped back to its peacetime size of eight thousand men. As before, there was no provision for retirement of officers, so that the younger men must wait for deaths or resignations in order to advance. At thirty years of age, Grant was still only a first lieutenant. The four years of fighting in Mexico had ended his dream of a teaching assignment at West Point and eventual professorship at a private university. Without the necessary academic background, he could not become a professor now. On his first lieutenant's pay he had not been able to save any money to go into business on his own. If he left the army, his only choice would be to return to Bethel and go into the tannery business with his father.

As the lesser of two evils Grant decided to remain in the service, even when he learned that the Fourth Infantry was being sent to the Pacific Coast. Many of the men were taking their families with them, but Julia was expecting another child. Grant would have to send for her and the children later. But fortunes were being made in California. Maybe out West he would find some new opportunity.

After escorting Julia to Bethel to remain with his parents, Grant returned to Governor's Island, New York, where his regiment was assembling prior to sailing. It was the beginning of a three-month nightmare. Arrangements had been made for

Between Wars

them to sail to the Isthmus of Panama aboard the steamer *Ohio* on July 5, but the ship was already packed with civilians. As quartermaster, Grant had the job of seeing that bunks were built on deck, stocking supplies and finding storage room for the regimental gear.

On July 16, they disembarked at Aspinwall and passengers and supplies were transferred to the Panama Pacific Railway for the first lap of their trip across the isthmus. Since the railway was still under construction, the tracks only went twenty miles inland to the crossing of the Chagres River. Here Grant arranged for passengers and gear to be transferred to dugout canoes, which would carry them up the river to the village of Cruces where they would continue on muleback the remaining twenty five miles to Panama City.

Each canoe, capable of carrying thirty to forty persons, was poled by several near-naked boatmen who raced up and down the flattened sides dipping their long poles into the murky water. At night while the women and children huddled in the canoes, the boatmen danced and caroused around their campfires on shore.

They were not alone on the river. Hundreds of civilians were traveling in the same direction, all bound for the California goldfields. At Cruces Grant had made arrangements with a contractor to supply them with mules at the standard rate of ten dollars apiece. When they reached the village, he found that the contractor had succumbed to the blandishments of the civilians and rented them all of his mules for forty dollars a head. Added to this catastrophe was news that an epidemic of Asiatic cholera had broken out in Panama City.

For several days Grant remained in Cruces haggling with the contractor. Some of his party became sick. Ordering the men to march ahead on foot, Grant arranged for women, children and the sick to be transported in hammocks carried by natives, while he brought up the rear with the few pack animals he had been able to find carrying their gear.

At Panama City, the steamer *Golden Gate* was waiting to carry them north, but the ship's captain refused to sail with cholera aboard. Those who were well were transferred to a camp on an isolated island in the bay. The ill were moved to an old vessel which was converted into a hospital ship, while the captain ordered the *Golden Gate* fumigated. His actions probably saved the lives of the rest of the regiment, but by the time they left the pestilence-ridden city on August 5, almost one third of the party had died. Among the dead was Captain Gore. As Grant made the arrangements for Mrs. Gore and her son to return home, he was suddenly thankful that he had not brought Julia with him.

On September 15, the *Golden Gate* finally reached San Francisco. Though it had been more than four years since James Marshall had discovered gold at Sutter's Mill, the city was still jammed with adventurers and gold seekers. Prices for food and lodging were exorbitant. Some of the troops left them here to go to scattered posts along the coast, but regimental headquarters were to be at Fort Vancouver on the Columbia River. As regimental quartermaster, Grant sailed north again, arriving at Fort Vancouver in late September. Located a hundred miles up the Columbia River, near the present city of Portland, Oregon, the fort had originally been a Hudson Bay Company trading post belonging to the British. Though the settlement of the boundary with Canada in 1846 had brought the post inside United States territory, it had been allowed to continue in operation. A village of huts inhabited by half-breed trappers and their families surrounded the original fort, while a new fort for the American soldiers had been built on a bluff a half mile back from the river.

To Grant's surprise he found Rufus Ingalls, his freshman roommate at West Point, already stationed at the fort. With

Ingalls and several other single officers he occupied a two-story frame building nicknamed "the Ranch." Later, when Ingalls was transferred to another post, Grant and the other officers invited a married sergeant to move in with them so that his wife could do their cooking.

The days seemed long and lonely without Julia. The mails were so slow that it was almost the end of the year before Grant learned of the birth of his second son, Ulysses Simpson Grant, Jr., the preceding July. As the rainy Oregon winter set in, Grant's homesickness became almost unbearable. He longed to send for Julia and the children but dreaded the thought of that dangerous crossing at the isthmus. Even if he had decided to send for them, he did not have the money for their passage.

Men were reported to be making fortunes in San Francisco. In the hopes of raising the money to bring his family to Oregon, Grant went into several business ventures with his fellow officers. He leased a piece of land and put in a crop of potatoes, only to lose most of it when the Columbia River overflowed. With another officer he bought up all the available chickens at Fort Vancouver and shipped them to San Francisco, but the ship ran into rough seas and the chickens died en route. Other attempts to ship hogs and even ice to San Francisco proved equally unsuccessful. Where other men were making money, Grant's business ventures all failed.

In September 1853, when he had been at Fort Vancouver a year, Grant received word that he had been promoted to captain and was to leave at once to take command of Company F, stationed at Fort Humboldt, California. Grant sailed to San Francisco where he boarded a smaller vessel that took him 250 miles back up the coast to Humboldt Bay and his new post. Fort Humboldt, located on a bluff overlooking the southern arm of the bay, had been built earlier that year. Except for a small lumber settlement farther up the bay, eventually Eureka, California, the area was even more sparsely settled than that around Fort Vancouver. Commanding the fort was Colonel Robert Buchanan, the martinet officer with whom Grant had tangled years before at Jefferson Barracks.

Buchanan and Grant had not liked each other in Missouri and now, in the closer confines of the small fort, they irritated each other even more. No longer busy with his quartermaster duties, Grant found the life of a line officer dull and boring. Since he did not care for hunting, he spent his spare time horseback riding, playing cards or drinking with the other officers. Still a stickler for rules and regulations, Buchanan particularly objected to the drinking.

If the mail service had seemed slow at Fort Vancouver, it was even more erratic at Fort Humboldt. Except for ships coming to pick up lumber, few vessels stopped at Humboldt Bay. Grant's letters home became increasingly despondent as he waited weeks on end with no word from Julia. He wondered how many more times in the future he would be separated from his wife and children. Though he was a captain now, there were nine other captains in the Fourth Regiment and it would be years before he could hope for another promotion.

Grant had received word of his promotion to captain in September 1853, but it was April 11, 1854, before his formal commission finally arrived. That same day Grant addressed two letters to the adjutant general. In the first, he acknowledged receipt of his commission; in the second, he tendered his resignation from the army.

Years later in his *Memoirs* he gave no real explanation for this decision. According to his grandson and biographer, Major General Ulysses S. Grant III, the action was the result of homesickness for his family and disillusionment over his chances for the future in the army. According to rumors that quickly spread among some of his fellow officers, the resignation was the result of a clash with Buchanan over his drinking. One account even went as far as to say Buchanan had demanded the resignation. Since there was no evidence that Grant had ever been derelict in his duties, the latter seems exaggerated, but when Grant ignored the rumors and made no reply to them, it was the beginning of a legend that would haunt him for the rest of his life.

Whatever the reason for the resignation, Buchanan accepted it readily. Relieved of duty on May 1, Grant sailed for San Francisco where he unsuccessfully tried to collect some money owed him. Continuing on to the isthmus, he arrived in New York penniless. Fortunately he ran into an old classmate, Simon Bolivar Buckner, who lent him the money to pay his hotel bill until Jesse could send the funds to get him to Bethel.

It was not the happy homecoming of former times. Jesse Grant had been shocked by the resignation. With his usual presumptuousness, he had written the War Department demanding that the resignation be turned down so that he could persuade his son to reconsider. In a rather cool reply, Secretary of War Jefferson Davis pointed out that since the resignation had been tendered by Grant and accepted, it was too late for a retraction. When Grant arrived, he found his family in the process of moving from Bethel to Covington, Kentucky, just across the Ohio River from Cincinnati. Staying only a few days, Grant hurried on to White Haven where Julia was living now with the two children.

At White Haven with Julia in his arms again, Grant felt he was really home at last. There were no questions from Julia or from Colonel Dent, who had disapproved of Grant's army career from the beginning. Temporarily Grant settled down at White Haven, getting reacquainted with his young sons.

Julia owned sixty acres of land on the Gravois Road which they decided Grant would farm. The land was heavily timbered so Grant spent that winter and the next spring felling trees and hauling the wood for sale in St. Louis. Occasionally he ran into old army friends. Observing his worn blue army coat and mudcaked farmer's boots, they wrote to other friends that Grant looked "seedy and run down." But Grant had never been one for fancy clothes. Just being with Julia and the boys was contentment. In July 1855, their first daughter, Ellen, was born. By the next summer they were able to move into their own home on the sixty acres. With a touch of wry humor, Grant named it Hardscrabble.

The name was well applied, for money was scarce. But it was not an unhappy time. The Grants visited with neighbors and attended local parties. Too poor to own a buggy, they traveled on horseback, carrying the children on the saddles ahead of them.

Millard Fillmore and Franklin Pierce had followed Zachary Taylor as President of the United States, but in the election of 1856, when the abolitionists caused a split in the Whig Party and John C. Frémont was the candidate of the newly formed Republican Party, Grant broke with his family's political background and voted for the Democrat, James Buchanan. Even a Democrat in the Presidency could not settle the mounting tension between North and South. In 1857 this unrest led to another financial panic. If the Grants were poor, so were many others. One day in St. Louis Grant ran into an old friend who looked as shabby as himself. It was Will Sherman, who had left the army for an unsuccessful try at banking in California and was as hard up as Grant.

Unhappily for Grant, conditions did not improve. When Mrs. Dent died and Colonel Dent moved into St. Louis, he and Julia leased out Hardscrabble and moved back to White Haven where a fourth child, Jesse Root Grant, was born. In 1858 a cold spell ruined their crop, then Grant was taken ill with a fever that laid him up for months. By 1859 he had to face the unpleasant fact that he was not going to succeed as a farmer. Moving into St. Louis, he made an unsuccessful attempt to sell real estate, failed in his efforts to get an appointment as county surveyor and worked briefly in the local customhouse. In 1860, at thirty-eight years of age, Grant finally gave in to the inevitable and returned north to join his father and brothers in the tannery business.

The move was not prompted entirely by financial difficulties. The differences between North and South were mounting rapidly and all Congressional attempts at compromises only seemed to make matters worse. The passage of the Fugitive Slave Act, which called for the return of slaves escaping to free territory, was considered an abomination by the North. Equally distasteful to the South was the admission of Kansas as a free state. But the final spark came on October 16, 1859, when John Brown, the fanatical abolitionist in whose home Jesse Grant had lived as a young man, attempted to seize the arsenal at Harpers Ferry, Virginia. When Brown was hanged on December 2, he became a martyr in the eyes of the North and the vilest of traitors in the eyes of the South.

Grant found himself a man in the middle. To his father, he was a Southern sympathizer. To the many Southern friends whom he had made over the years, he was suddenly suspect as a born Northerner and former Whig. The situation in the South became intolerable. "It made my blood run cold to hear friends of mine, Southern men—as many of my friends were—deliberately discuss the dissolution of the Union as though it were a tariff bill. I could not endure it. . . ." he wrote.

So in 1860 Grant, Julia and the children moved north to Galena, Illinois, where Grant joined his two younger brothers in operating a new store owned by their father. Though Grant did not shirk his duties, he found clerking in a store almost as distasteful as working in the tannery. More enjoyable were the frequent business trips he made into the neighboring states of Indiana and Wisconsin. But as he traveled about the country, he was dismayed to find there was as much war talk in the North as there had been back in Missouri.

Following in their father's footsteps, Grant's brother Orvil was active in the Galena Republican organization, along with the local Congressman, Elihu B. Washburne. Shortly after moving to Galena, Grant became close friends with John A. Rawlins, a handsome and eloquent young lawyer who was an active Democrat. But Grant remained in the middle, refusing to affiliate with either party. Deep in his heart he clung to the hope that the Southern states would not be so suicidal as to attempt to leave the Union.

The election of Abraham Lincoln to the Presidency that fall ended all hope of reconciliation. On December 20, South Carolina seceded, followed by Mississippi and Florida. Eventually eleven states seceded from the Union. On March 4, 1861, Lincoln was sworn into office. Fort Sumter, in the harbor at Charleston, South Carolina, was fired upon by the Confederate forces on April 12, and the war began. When the news reached Washington, Lincoln immediately issued a call for 75,000 volunteers to serve for ninety days.

On April 15, the news of the fall of Fort Sumter reached the telegraph office at Galena. That night Grant accompanied Orvil to a town meeting attended largely by Republicans. Three nights later they attended another town meeting where Rawlins got up and made a stirring speech calling for Northern Republicans and Democrats to unite in fighting to preserve the Union. Later that evening as Grant and his brother walked home through the darkness, they discussed the situation. They agreed that it was Orvil's duty as the second oldest son to remain home to attend the family business while Grant, because of his previous army experience, must return to the service. As to just where and how he would return, Grant was undecided.

Chapter VI

Back in Harness

That next week Grant helped recruit and organize a volunteer company from Galena, but he refused to act as their captain, believing that his service would be more valuable elsewhere. On April 26, he accompanied the company to Springfield, saw them registered at Camp Yates where the Illinois Volunteers were being assembled and checked into the Cherney Hotel, planning to return to Galena in the morning.

Grant's table for dinner that night was near that of the governor of Illinois, Richard Yates, for whom the training camp had been named. As Grant was leaving the dining room, Yates asked him to come to his office the next morning. Impressed by the recruitment work being done at Galena, Yates had been making inquiries about Grant and receiving confusing answers. Some of those he questioned cited Grant's dependability. Others, recalling the rumors surrounding Grant's resignation, said he had reached the end of the line as far as military usefulness was concerned.

Yates liked to make his own judgments. At the following day's interview, he asked Grant to act as his personal adjutant in charge of all the Illinois recruiting. For a month Grant traveled about Illinois, organizing local companies and seeing them transported to Camp Yates, but it was only a temporary position. Near the end of May, with most of the mustering in completed, he returned to Galena.

By now President Lincoln had issued a new call for 300,000 volunteers to serve for three years. On May 24, Grant responded by writing to the adjutant general and volunteering his services. Weeks passed and he received no reply. Learning that George B. McClellan had been appointed major general in charge of the Ohio district, which also included Indiana and Illinois, Grant traveled to Cincinnati to offer his services to McClellan personally. For two days he waited in an outer office, but McClellan was too busy to see him. Failing in his second attempt to get back into the army, there was nothing for Grant to do but return to Galena.

Those early months of the war were a time of confusion for both the North and the South as they struggled to marshal their forces. By now eleven states had seceded, the most painful loss being Virginia, which Lincoln had hoped would at least remain neutral. An equally severe loss had been that of the brilliant Robert E. Lee. Now that Zachary Taylor was dead and Winfield Scott too old for active service, Lincoln had hoped to make Lee commander in chief. As officers were shifted about and hundreds of politically important civilians clamored for top commands in the volunteers, the modest request of former Captain Grant went unnoticed.

If the regular army refused to appreciate Grant's potential, Governor Yates was of a different opinion. With the ninety-day enlistments drawing to a close, every effort was being made to get the volunteers to continue on for a three-year term. The 21st Illinois regiment, made up of rambunctious farm youths from east central Illinois, was giving Yates trouble. From an enlistment of 1250 their ranks had thinned to six hundred. With their roistering and carousing in town, they had won the nickname "Yate's Hellions," and already forced one inex-

Back in Harness

perienced colonel to resign. In mid-September Yates wrote to Grant offering him command of the 21st.

On September 16, Grant returned to Camp Yates. There had not been time to order a colonel's uniform and he was dressed in civilian clothes, a shabby coat patched at the elbows and an old plug hat. The men of the 21st, expecting someone more impressive, could not conceal their disappointment. As Grant strolled down the line of tents, there was snickering and some of the bolder youths fell in behind him, pretending to spar at his back. In the course of these antics, one slipped and landed a blow between Grant's shoulder blades that knocked off the plug hat. Without a word, Grant retrieved the hat and turned to give his antagonists such a cool stare that they fell back in consternation.

Continuing on to his command tent, Grant tossed his hat on a chair and announced he was getting to work. Soon a flurry of orders issued from the tent. The nightly guard posted to keep the men from running away to town was removed and the soldiers were given exact hours to report for roll call. New rules were set down and intensive drilling began. Within a week the recalcitrants were beginning to shape up and Grant had been dubbed, with new respect "the quiet man."

Grant did not have much time in which to work. June 28 had been set as the date when the men would be asked to reenlist for three years. Two Democratic Congressmen, John A. Logan and John A. McClernand, were sent to assist Grant with their oratory. Their speeches were so eloquent that the entire regiment reenlisted almost to a man and there were demands that Grant should also give a speech. He responded with one of the shortest recruiting speeches on record. "Go to your quarters, men," he ordered, the tone of his voice leaving no doubt that the time for oratory was over and the job of being soldiers had begun.

So far no major battles had taken place, but sporadic fighting had erupted along the border between the North and the South and particularly in Missouri, which had remained neutral. On July 3, Grant received orders to move his regiment to Quincy, Illinois, one hundred miles to the west on the Mississippi River. Customarily troops were transported by train, but having ten days to reach his destination, Grant decided to march his men to Quincy on foot to give them added training.

They got off to a late start, making only five miles the first day. As they bivouacked for the night, Grant gave orders that the march would resume at six the next morning. When the bugles sounded at 6 A.M., some of the companies were still sleeping and others had barely started their breakfast fires. Grant said nothing as again they covered only five miles. That night Grant issued the same orders for the march to resume at 6 A.M. The next morning when the bugles sounded, the camp was in the same somnolent state of unpreparedness. Without a word, Grant mounted his horse and with a few aides started on his way, leaving the entire regiment behind him in frantic confusion as men struggled into their clothes, cooks doused their fires and officers bellowed orders to get packed. It was afternoon before the last of the stragglers, unfed and with their gear slammed together every which way, caught up with their commander. That night Grant repeated the same orders. The next morning as he mounted his horse, he noted with satisfaction that every man was fed, packed and waiting to fall in.

The trip to Quincy did not continue all the way on foot. En route, Grant received orders to go to the assistance of a besieged Union regiment in Missouri. When Grant had returned from Galena to take command, he had brought his eldest son, Fred, with him to give the boy a taste of military life. Now, with the prospect of fighting immediately ahead, he cut back to the railroad where he sent Fred home and commandeered cars to hurry his regiment on to Quincy. There was no need for the rush. When they reached their destination, they found that the supposedly trapped regiment had already escaped and reached Quincy ahead of them.

For several weeks Grant and his regiment were deployed along the Salt River guarding railway lines; then in late July orders came to move south to Florida, Missouri, where a Confederate force under Colonel Thomas Harris was encamped. During most of the Mexican War, Grant had been unaware of any fear when moving into battle, but as he led his men south past deserted farmhouses, abandoned in anticipation of the coming battle, he was aware of that same nervous tightening in his chest that he had felt when he marched out of Point Isabel toward his first encounter with the Mexicans at Palo Alto. He recognized it now as due to the responsibility of his first major command and he found himself wishing that he was only a captain again. But when he came over the crest of the hills, on the other side of which the enemy was supposedly waiting, he saw only the deserted campground where they had been the night before. Warned of his approach, the Confederate colonel had withdrawn.

Though there had been no fighting, Grant considered the march to Florida one of his most valuable experiences of the war. "It occurred to me at once that Harris had been as much afraid of me as I had been of him," he wrote later in his *Memoirs*. "This was a view of the question that I had never taken before and one I never forgot afterward. From that event to the close of the war I never experienced trepidation upon confronting an enemy. . . . I never forgot that he had as much reason to fear my forces as I had his."

Grant's chance to test this new assurance did not come immediately. At about the same time he had been marching south against Harris, the first major battle of the war had taken place in northern Virginia. The first battle of Bull Run on July 21 had been a resounding defeat for the Union forces. With the nation's attention focused on major eastern battles, the war in the West continued to be one of sporadic encounters between small units. Commanding the Union forces in Missouri was Major General John C. Frémont. Though Frémont had distinguished himself as a young officer for his explorations of the West and his assistance in taking California during the Mexican War, he was not experienced when it came to a large-scale war. Eccentric and flamboyant, he maintained his headquarters at St. Louis with great pomp and ceremony but accomplished little in organizing a decisive campaign plan.

Following the Florida march, Grant was stationed at Mexico, Missouri, where he spent his time drilling two new regiments that had been added to his command. In the twenty years since he had last studied tactics at West Point, the army had made changes. They were now using a new book, a translation of French procedure written by William J. Hardee, one of the leading generals of the Confederate forces. Determined not to appear out of date, Grant secured Hardee's book. "I got a copy of tactics and studied one lesson, intending to confine the exercises of the first day to the commands I had thus learned. By pursuing this course from day to day, I thought I would soon get through the volume," he wrote in his *Memoirs*.

Grant got no further than that first chapter. When he assembled his men to put them through the first lesson, he found to his chagrin that the drill field was too small for the grand-scale maneuvers described in the book. He was forced to improvise on the spot. After hastily glancing through the remainder of the book that night, he continued improvising, relying on what he already knew and ordinary common sense. "I do not believe that the officers of the regiments ever discovered that I had never studied the tactics I used," he added.

On August 7, Grant was sitting in his headquarters when a regimental chaplain rushed in waving a copy of a St. Louis newspaper. According to an account in the paper, President Lincoln had promoted Grant to the rank of brigadier general.

Back in Harness

Unfortunately, the promotion was not a sign of recognition by the regular army. From the beginning, Grant had refused to seek advancement by currying political favor, but his appointment was political nevertheless. Learning that Lincoln planned to give several brigadier generalships to the Illinois Volunteers, Congressman Elihu Washburne had put up Grant's name in order to secure one of the appointments for his district.

With the arrival of his formal papers, Grant was moved again. He spent several weeks at Ironton and Jefferson City, Missouri. To his disappointment, each time he was about to lead his troops into battle, he was replaced by another general. On August 28, he learned that he was being given command of southern Illinois and southeastern Missouri with headquarters at Cairo, Illinois. No assignment could have pleased him more.

If the secession of Virginia had been a blow to the North, the establishment of the Confederate capital at Richmond was the final insult. Following the defeat at Bull Run, the eastern Army of the Potomac was being reorganized completely and the leading generals in Washington with bullheaded determination continued concentrating their war strategy on the capture of Richmond.

Grant did not agree. He still clung to an optimistic hope that the South would come to its senses and the war would be of short duration. But if it continued for any length of time, he was convinced that control of the Mississippi River would be the key to final victory. Though railways laced everywhere across the eastern and southern states, the Mississippi River and its tributaries were still the great transportation artery for both the North and the South. Whoever controlled the Mississippi would eventually win the war.

Cairo, located at the junction of the Ohio and Mississippi Rivers at the far southern tip of Illinois, occupied the most strategic location of any Union city on the river. Across the Mississippi to the east was Missouri; across the Ohio to the south was Kentucky, making Cairo the natural jumping-off point for any move south.

Though a busy port, Cairo was far from attractive as a city. It was located behind high levees that held back both rivers, and the streets were constantly muddy despite the round-the-clock working of pumps. Everywhere there were mosquitoes, flies, dysentery and malaria, and the waterfront was so overrun with rats that sentries walking between posts amused themselves by seeing how many they could spear with their swords. In the estimation of one newspaper reporter, the townspeople were little better. "If the Angel Gabriel should alight there, the natives would steal his trumpet before he could blow it," he wrote.

On receiving his promotion, Grant had laid aside his colonel's uniform but had not found time to secure a general's uniform. He arrived in Cairo on September 4, wearing his shabby civilian coat and an old slouch hat. The headquarters were jammed with officers, all demanding the attention of the commanding colonel. With the briefest glance at the unimpressive newcomer, the colonel ignored him completely. It was not until Grant seated himself at a table and quietly started issuing orders of his own that the chagrined officer realized that his superior had arrived.

If Lincoln's advisers in Washington still failed to see the importance of a Mississippi campaign, the Confederate commanders realized that the Mississippi River was the life blood of the South. Like Missouri, Kentucky had sought to remain neutral, but shortly before Grant reached Cairo, the South had invaded Kentucky by sending Major General Gideon Pillow to seize Columbus, Kentucky, on the Mississippi River about twenty miles downstream from Cairo. Two days after Grant reached Cairo a scout brought word that Pillow was sending troops overland to seize Paducah, forty-five miles east of Cairo

Back in Harness

on the Ohio River, a move that could give the Confederates control of virtually all western Kentucky.

On hearing this news, Grant sent a wire to Frémont: "Unless I hear from you to the contrary, I shall move on Paducah tonight." He sent another telegram to the Kentucky legislature informing them of the necessity for him to move into their territory.

Loading two regiments of infantry and one battery of artillery onto transports, Grant waited impatiently until midnight. When no reply came from Frémont, he gave orders to cast off and accompanied by three small wooden-sided gunboats, started up the Ohio. By dawn they had reached the junction of the Tennessee and Ohio Rivers where Paducah was located. Putting ashore, they took the city without opposition. The majority of the townspeople remained locked in their houses. The few who were about were busy hauling down Confederate flags with which they had been planning to greet the expected Confederate forces. As it turned out the Confederate soldiers were only a few miles away, but hearing that Paducah had been occupied, they withdrew to Columbus.

Leaving two gunboats and enough troops to hold the town, Grant returned to Cairo where he found a telegram from Frémont, giving him permission to move on Paducah. It was followed by two more telegrams, one rebuking him for his unauthorized move in contacting the Kentucky legislature and the other informing him that General Charles F. Smith, who had been commandant of cadets when Grant was at West Point, was taking command at Paducah.

Ignoring these two rather obvious rebuffs, Grant sent off a telegram of his own, requesting permission to move downstream and wrest Columbus away from Pillow. Grant remembered Pillow from the Mexican War as a gallant but inept political opportunist who had arrived in camp so ill-versed in military matters that he had ordered his regiment to throw up their breastwork facing in the wrong direction. Grant felt that if Pillow was still as inept today, he would be an easy opponent. Not sharing Grant's optimism, Frémont ordered him to remain where he was.

Temporarily there was nothing more Grant could do. He took lodgings in the Cairo Hotel and set up his headquarters in a brick bank building, where he went about the business of purchasing supplies, providing for the drilling of the new troops arriving daily and directing the construction of fortifications along the Kentucky shoreline of the Ohio River. By now his uniform had arrived, but even in uniform he presented an unprepossessing appearance, being inclined to sloppiness in dress, with a long, unkempt beard and a stained meerschaum pipe continually dangling from his mouth. Brigade Surgeon John H. Brinton, who joined Grant in Cairo, described their first meeting:

> As I first saw him, he was a very short, small, rather spare man with full beard and moustache. His beard was a little long, much longer than he afterwards wore it, unkempt and irregular, and of a sandy, tawny shade. His hair matched his beard, and at first glance he seemed to be a very ordinary sort of man, indeed one below the average in most respects. But as I sat and watched him then, and many an hour afterwards, I found that his face grew on me. His eyes were gentle with a kind expression, and thoughtful. He did not, as a rule, speak a great deal. . . .

Also arriving in Cairo as Grant's personal aide was Captain John A. Rawlins, the young lawyer who had been Grant's friend back in Galena. With his promotion to brigadier general Grant had been given the right to select his personal aides. Of all the men who served on his staff, Rawlins was the one who would become the closest to Grant and remain with him throughout the war. Not yet thirty years of age, Rawlins was arrestingly handsome with swarthy skin, dark hair and flashing black eyes. Like Grant, he was a man of action. Grant's years of experience as a quartermaster had given him a thorough knowledge of buying and outfitting, but he hated bookkeeping. His method of filing reports, letters and receipts was to keep shoving them into his pockets until they bulged like a chipmunk's cheek pouches, then empty the whole mess onto a table. Rawlins took over the task of seeing that these papers were properly filed. Inclined to be domineering, Rawlins bossed everyone and loudly cursed out those who annoyed him, including Grant himself if he thought the general was at fault. To everyone's surprise Grant shrugged off these tongue-lashings with an amused grin and the friendship persisted.

Another friend of Grant's was youthful Flag Officer Andrew Foote, in charge of the navy gunboats at Cairo, who shared Grant's belief that their superiors were being too cautious in proceeding against the enemy. In early November Grant and Foote finally had their chance. While Grant had been gathering troops at Cairo, General Pillow had been similarly engaged building up his forces at Columbus. Now word came that the Confederates were planning to send soldiers across the Mississippi River to cut off the regiments Grant had operating in eastern Missouri. Until the navy could send Foote some of the new ironclad gunboats that were being constructed, Grant was forbidden to attempt a major assault on Columbus, but he received orders to proceed down the Mississippi and make some kind of demonstration that might discourage the shipment of troops across the river.

On November 6, with five regiments of infantry, two heavy guns and two companies of cavalry, accompanied by two gunboats, Grant started down the river. His men were fretting for action. Columbus, situated on a high bluff where its guns could sweep the water below, was practically invulnerable to attack from the river, but directly across the Mississippi at the small settlement of Belmont several Confederate regiments had set up a temporary camp. As the boats lay several miles upriver on the morning of November 7, Grant in his headquarters aboard the *Belle Memphis* made an abrupt decision. He had orders not to attack Columbus, but nothing had been said about Belmont.

Later he wrote:

> I had no orders which contemplated an attack by the national troops, nor did I intend anything of the kind when I started out from Cairo; but after we started I saw that the officers and men were elated at the prospect of at last having the opportunity of doing what they had volunteered to do—fight the enemies of their country. I did not see how I could maintain discipline, or retain the confidence of my command, if we should return to Cairo without an effort to do something.

Putting ashore north of Belmont, Grant landed 2500 troops and started south through tall cornfields, then on into rolling, wooded country. About three miles out of Belmont the alerted Confederates opened fire and the battle began. In view of later battles, Grant's first command under fire was handled clumsily. He left insufficient reserves behind him and moved his men forward in a single long line that could have been easily broken by a concentrated charge of the enemy. But General Pillow, living up to Grant's estimate of his abilities, was equally clumsy. Grant's men fought their way forward from tree to tree, scrambled over an abatis of felled and sharpened tree trunks that protected the perimeter of the camp and forced the Confederates to flee for the river.

If the Union soldiers had pushed their advantage, they might have won a decisive victory. Instead, elated with their unex-

Back in Harness

pected success, Grant's raw troops went wild, running through the deserted camp looting and searching for souvenirs. Reaching the river and finding they were not being pursued, the Confederates did not take to their boats, but signaled to their comrades across the river at Columbus to send reinforcements, directing them to the north where they could cut Grant off from returning to his ships.

In vain, Grant tried to alert his rioting troops to the danger. Finally in order to get their attention, he directed Rawlins and his other aides to set fire to the camp. As the soldiers realized what was happening, there was momentary panic and cries of "We're surrounded! . . . What are we going to do?"

"Fight our way back through them the same way we got in," Grant replied grimly. With order restored, the battle resumed and they fought their way back to the boats. Bringing up the rear, Grant was momentarily cut off from the others. As a Confederate company marched by along a road a few feet away, he hid in a cornfield. Once they were gone, he galloped out around them and as the last man up the gangplank of the *Belle Memphis,* he gave orders to cast off. Exhausted, Grant climbed to the top deck and threw himself on a sofa in the salon. Hearing musket fire from the bank, he rose to see what was going on. As he reached the door, a musket ball tore through the planking of the cabin and buried itself in the sofa where he had been resting seconds before.

The following day, when Grant met with Confederate officers on a truce boat in midstream to arrange for burial of the dead and exchange of the wounded, he could not resist telling them how he had watched them from the cornfield. To his surprise, he learned that one of the officers had seen him and pointed him out to his men. "There is a Yankee; you may try your marksmanship on him if you wish," he had said. Because he had been wearing an ordinary soldier's coat, Grant had not been recognized and none of the Confederate soldiers had accepted the challenge to use him for a target.

Belmont was claimed as a victory by the South and conceded as such by most of the North. Grant did not share this opinion, pointing out that his men had achieved their objective since no more Confederate troops were sent across the river.

The action at Belmont had not endeared Grant to his superiors. By rushing off to take Paducah without waiting for Frémont's orders and by the unnecessary risks at Belmont, he had shown himself to be reckless. However, he drew no rebuke. He was too minor an officer to elicit much concern in Washington, where more important matters occupied everyone's attention. The aged Winfield Scott had been removed from top command of the army with George B. McClellan moved up to replace him. In Missouri, Frémont was replaced by Henry Wager Halleck, a brilliant tactician and textbook general with the nickname of "Old Brains." Don Carlos Buell, who had attended West Point along with Grant, was given command of eastern Kentucky. The Union was placing great hopes on this triumvirate of McClellan, Halleck and Buell, who were considered the most able strategists available. Almost immediately all three had the wires humming as they sought to perfect a master plan to be used against the South.

Meanwhile, Grant fretted at Cairo. Looking over the purchases being made by his command, he was appalled at the profiteering. He started canceling government contracts and purchasing his own supplies on the open market. Since the majority of the contractors had gained their contracts through political influence, he stepped on important toes. Among those who had contracts canceled was Leonard Swett, a powerful political figure who owned a controlling interest in the Illinois Central Railroad and had been responsible for putting Lincoln's name in nomination at the Republican convention. Swett threatened to go to the President. "Go tell him then," Grant replied.

Back in Harness

When Swett continued to bluster, Grant gave him twenty-four hours to get out of Illinois and added a final warning that, if he ever saw him again, he might shoot him.

Swett lost no time in reporting this treatment to Lincoln. But Lincoln had begun to hear from others of this impatient general in Cairo, who believed in carrying the fight to the enemy. When Swett added that Grant as a final indignity had threatened to shoot him if he returned to Cairo, Lincoln observed dryly, "In that case, you'd better stay out of Illinois; from what I've heard of this Grant, he is just the man who might do it."

By now the strategy of the Confederate generals had become obvious. They had thrown up a strong defensive line across Kentucky, from Columbus on the Mississippi River, east 140 miles to Bowling Green. Bisecting this line north and south were two major rivers, the Cumberland and the Tennessee, which flowed from Tennessee north across Kentucky to empty into the Ohio. Just inside the Tennessee border, guarding any movement up these rivers and into the South, were two forts, Fort Henry on the Tennessee and Fort Donelson twelve miles to the east on the Cumberland. With its strategic position on a high bluff overlooking the river, Fort Donelson was a strong emplacement. Fort Henry, being located on lower ground, was considerably weaker since its lower guns were subject to seasonal flooding. To rectify this weakness, the Confederates were in the process of building a second fort, Fort Heiman, across the river.

Early in January, when it was learned that Confederate General Simon B. Buckner was receiving heavy reinforcements at Bowling Green, it was decided to send Buell against him. However, before he got underway, Grant was ordered to make a feint toward Fort Henry in an effort to mislead the Confederates into believing that the Union strike would be there. This time Grant obeyed orders. Accompanied by several of the new ironclad gunboats and a token force of troops, he steamed up the Tennessee River, exchanged a few shots with Fort Henry and withdrew. But when Grant got back to Cairo, nothing could quell his excitement over what he had seen. Due to flooding, Fort Henry was practically awash; Fort Heiman was in only the beginning stages of construction, and he felt both could be taken with ease. This time he did not send a wire but took off for St. Louis in person to ask Halleck's permission to move against Fort Henry.

Halleck had little confidence in Grant's ability as a strategist. Snubbing him coldly, he denied the request. Back in Cairo, Grant's enthusiasm for the project was undiminished. Flag Officer Foote shared his conviction that Fort Henry could be taken easily and late in January they individually sent new requests to move up the Tennessee. Though Grant held little hope that the permission would be granted, unknown to him, army politics was coming to his aid. Buell and Halleck were bitterly jealous of each other. At the eastern end of the state in the Cumberland Mountains, one of the generals serving under Buell had just won a decisive victory. If Buell continued with a successful push against Bowling Green, all the credit for the victory in Kentucky would go to him. Halleck realized he had to get some of his own men into the field and on February 1, he got off a telegram to Grant telling him to proceed against Fort Henry.

The affirmative reply was so unexpected that there was a moment of stunned silence when it reached Grant's headquarters. Then men went wild, cheering, stamping and tossing their hats into the air. The paper war was over; they were heading south!

Chapter VII

The Pendulum of War

Loading his men onto every ship available, Grant left Cairo on March 3, 1862, accompanied by Foote and seven gunboats, including four new ironclads. There was no chance for secrecy as the flotilla moved up the Tennessee River. The ship's stacks belched a pall of black smoke that could be seen for miles, due to the pitch pine being burned in the boilers, and Kentuckians lined the banks to watch them pass.

The transporting of troops took longer than expected because of the shortage of vessels. Landing the men from Cairo nine miles below Fort Henry, Grant left them in charge of General John McClernand, the former Congressman who had helped him so eloquently with the recruiting at Camp Yates, and steamed back down the river to pick up General Smith and his division from Paducah. When the troops finally assembled below Fort Henry on March 6, they numbered approximately fifteen thousand men. Grant sent Smith's division to take Fort Heiman on the other side of the river, while he and McClernand spread into the hills surrounding Fort Henry, and Foote moved his gunboats to attack from the river. With construction still uncompleted, the Confederates had withdrawn from Fort Heiman and Smith found it deserted. Before

Grant's men could reach the gun pits on the outer perimeter of Fort Henry, they heard the opening salvos from Foote's gunboats. Aware that they could not hold the half-flooded fort, the Confederates had withdrawn from Fort Henry also, leaving only a token force to man the guns. By the time Grant's troops reached the fort, it had already surrendered.

Sending off a wire to Halleck, in which he gave Foote credit for the victory, Grant said: "Fort Henry is ours. . . . I shall take and destroy Fort Donelson on the eighth and return to Fort Henry." The telegram caused both rejoicing and consternation at Halleck's headquarters. They had not expected such an easy victory, but according to the tactics worked out on paper, Grant could not possibly take Donelson without reinforcements. Halleck sent a wire ordering Grant to remain at Fort Henry until more men could reach him. More telegrams sped east to McClellan and Buell, as they tried to decide whether Buell or Halleck should be the one to go to Grant's assistance.

The dickering amounted to little. Either having failed to receive or ignoring Halleck's orders, Grant was already preparing to move. His estimate of taking Fort Donelson on the eighth was overly optimistic. The next day when he rode across the twelve-mile strip that separated the two forts to make a personal reconnaissance, Grant found Fort Donelson a more formidable target than Fort Henry. Its gun emplacements on bluffs one hundred feet above the river would have a heavy advantage over gunboats attacking from below. To the north and the south, it was protected by deep ravines flooded by overflow from the river. On the west, long lines of rifle pits and the usual abatis of felled trees extended out for several miles.

Though Grant planned to march his men overland to the fort, the gunboats would have a much longer journey, back down the Tennessee River, then up the Cumberland. Due to bad weather and the necessity of giving the gunboats time to get in position, the march overland did not start until March 12.

The Pendulum of War

Expecting to be in battle within a few hours, many of the soldiers threw away their overcoats and blankets. Grant traveled light also, taking only a toothbrush which he shoved into one of his bulging pockets and a clean collar which he entrusted to an aide.

It was dusk before they reached the western edge of the fort's perimeter. Following the same strategy he had used at Fort Henry, Grant ordered them spread out in a long semicircle completely surrounding the fort on the landward side, with McClernand's division to the south and Smith's to the north. There was no need to dig pits as the low hills formed a natural protection, but as the men settled around their fires in the bitter cold, many regretted the loss of their blankets.

By morning only one gunboat had appeared and the action was confined to minor skirmishing. Then two thousand reinforcements arrived under the command of Colonel John Thayer, they were placed in the center of the line between Smith's and McClernand's divisions, bringing Grant's strength to about seventeen thousand men. Inside Fort Donelson the Confederates had about 21,000, including the combined forces of General John B. Floyd, commander of the fort, the division from Columbus commanded by Pillow, and reinforcements from Bowling Green under General Simon B. Buckner. But as Grant rode out along the line that evening, he was in unusually jovial and optimistic spirits.

That night it was cold again, with a driving rain that turned to sleet by morning. The soldiers spent much of the night stamping around the fires and beating their arms to keep from freezing. By morning more gunboats had arrived and shortly after dawn Foote moved up the river with the four ironclads to open the attack. The advantage of the fort's guns on the high cliffs was too much. Soon the decks of the gunboats were red with blood and fires were breaking out. Foote's flagship, the *St. Louis,* was hit almost sixty times. The pilothouse was blown away and Foote himself was seriously wounded. From the surrounding hills, the Union soldiers watched in dismay as one by one the disabled ships drifted helplessly back down the river.

The next morning at his headquarters in a farmhouse west of the lines, Grant received word that Foote wanted to see him but was too badly injured to come in person. Mounting his horse, Grant took off immediately for the river where a small boat carried him out to the flagship. Here he learned from Foote that not one of the gunboats was left in fighting condition. Foote offered to float them back to Cairo for repairs, promising he could return in ten days. This would mean a siege and Grant was not ready to give up the initial attack this early. He started back to join his infantry.

While conferring with Foote, he had heard gunfire off to the south which grew steadily louder. Reaching the lines, he came upon a scene of milling confusion. Since they held a strong defensive position inside the fort, Grant had not expected the Confederates to charge, but early that morning they had attacked McClernand's forces on the south, breaking through the lines when the Union soldiers ran out of ammunition. Frantic word had been rushed to Grant's headquarters. When it was discovered he was not there, no one had acted to give orders. Finally, Colonel Thayer had rushed to fill the gap, but they were barely holding. Grant seemed unruffled. There was plenty of ammunition and he ordered it brought up immediately. Something about his calmness as he rode among the men restored order. With muskets reloaded, they rushed back to the fighting. From one of the soldiers Grant learned that the Confederate soldiers had been carrying full packs.

In Grant's eyes this could only mean that the Confederates had not been aiming to defeat his forces but to escape. If this was true, they would have most of their strength massed on the side of the fort leading to the roads to the south. Galloping

The Pendulum of War

back up the lines, Grant found General Smith resting under a tree and gave him orders to mount a full-scale attack from the north. Within minutes Smith had his men in action. By nightfall they had forced their way well inside the fort's grounds.

In the day's fighting the toll had been heavy on both sides. As Grant rode back toward his headquarters, he was sickened by the carnage. At one place along the road a severely wounded Union officer and a Confederate private lay side by side. With one arm around the private's neck, the Union officer was trying to give him water from his canteen. Halting, Grant ordered both men given a sip of brandy, then, as stretcher bearers arrived to pick up the officer, Grant told them to take the Confederate also. "Take them both together; the war is over between them," he said.

Arriving at his headquarters, Grant stretched out on a mattress on the kitchen floor. At dawn he was awakened by General Smith stamping into the kitchen. For a moment Smith appeared more concerned about his boots which had been badly scorched while he was trying to keep warm during the night, but finally he handed Grant a note which had been delivered to the front lines. During the night the Confederate generals Floyd and Pillow had managed to escape the fort with about four thousand men, leaving Buckner behind in command of the others. The note was from Buckner asking for peace terms.

Buckner was a long-time friend of Grant's, the officer who had so generously lent him money when he returned penniless from California. But this was war. Grant hastily wrote a reply which was to become famous:

> Sir: Yours of this date proposing Armistice and appointment of Commissioners to settle terms of Capitulation is just received. No terms except unconditional and immediate surrender can be accepted. . . .

A short time later Grant received Buckner's reply, calling Grant's terms "ungenerous" and "unchivalrous" but accepting them. Fort Donelson had fallen.

Buckner's reply had been somewhat irritable, but later that day he and Grant greeted each other like old friends. As they dined together, Buckner remarked wryly that the fort would not have fallen so easily if he had been in command.

Wiping his mouth on a napkin, Grant regarded him with a twinkle in his blue eyes. "I wouldn't have used the same tactics if you had been in command," he explained. Before they parted, Grant asked if Buckner had enough money and begged him to draw on his own account for what he might need during the period ahead when he would be a prisoner of war.

Back in St. Louis, Halleck was still conferring with Buell and McClellan about the course to be taken in assisting Grant when word reached him of Fort Donelson's surrender. In his jubilation over the victory, Halleck was willing to overlook the fact that Grant once again had ignored orders. He sent an immediate request to Lincoln that Buell, Grant and Smith be given promotions and suggested that he himself be given top command over the entire west. Lincoln had a mind of his own. Though he had never met Grant, he was beginning to like what he heard about this general who believed in carrying the fight to the enemy. As a result of the action at Fort Donelson, he sent only one request to Congress—for the promotion of U. S. Grant to major general with command of the army that was hereafter to be designated the Army of the Tennessee.

As news of the victory spread north, the until now almost unknown General U. S. Grant became the hero of the hour. It was the first major Union victory with strategic result. Western Kentucky was now in Union hands and the Union army well inside the state of Tennessee. It was also the single largest capture of men and arms since the start of the war, with 2500 Confederate soldiers killed and 14,623 taken prisoner.

The Pendulum of War

The public particularly liked Grant's reply to Buckner and he was given a new nickname, "Unconditional Surrender" Grant. Though ordinarily a pipe smoker, when Grant had left the conference aboard the flagship, Foote had handed him a cigar. Grant shoved it in his mouth, where it remained unlighted throughout the day's fighting. Several newspaper correspondents sent drawings of the battle back to their papers showing Grant sitting astride his horse with a cigar in his mouth and from all over the North a grateful public began sending the general boxes of cigars. Grant distributed many among his officers and, being a thrifty man, shoved the rest in his pockets intending to smoke them eventually. The habit became fixed and for the rest of his life he was seldom seen or pictured without a cigar.

The victory at Fort Donelson was a crippling blow to the South. Within a few days Nashville and Columbus were evacuated, with Memphis following a short time later. Grant wanted to push on south, believing that with aggressive action the war might be won that year. To his disgust, those higher in command were still committed to working everything out cautiously in advance on paper. On one point Grant and Halleck were in agreement. Both believed that the Union army suffered from having too many chiefs and Halleck continued his requests that the entire operation in the west be unified under his command. When this promotion did not appear, he took some of his irritation out on Grant. As he moved about between Fort Donelson, Fort Henry and Nashville, Grant's communications with St. Louis frequently bogged down. Halleck sent a complaint to McClellan charging Grant with ignoring orders and failing to send regular reports. McClellan curtly wired back that, if Grant was guilty of misconduct, Halleck should bring charges against him. With no real basis for formal charges, Halleck tried a new approach. He had heard the long-standing rumors about Grant's drinking and wired McClellan that there were rumors that "Grant had resumed his former habits." The situation became so difficult that Grant asked to be relieved. Happily all was resolved when Halleck received the long-desired appointment as commander in chief of the armies of the West. In a more expansive mood, he wrote Grant a conciliatory letter and informed the War Department that it all had been a misunderstanding.

By early 1862, Jefferson Davis had been formally inaugurated as president of the Confederate States. In the East, McClellan had left his desk in Washington to take personal command of the reorganized Army of the Potomac facing General Robert E. Lee. In the West, the Confederate generals Albert S. Johnston and P. T. Beauregard had been forced to move their defensive line south and were massing their strength at Corinth, Mississippi, an important railway junction ten miles west of the Tennessee River. According to reports, they had about forty thousand soldiers. Grant, with approximately the same number of men under his command, requested permission to march against them.

Halleck agreed, but with his usual caution wanted the Union forces to have numerical superiority. Grant was ordered to move down the Tennessee to some point above Corinth and wait there to be reinforced by Buell's Army of the Ohio, which was stationed at Nashville, while Halleck would join them later to take personal command. Proceeding down the river from Fort Henry in March with 35,000 men, Grant put shore at Pittsburg Landing twenty miles north of Corinth. The landing consisted of a single log building and docking facilities for riverboats at the base of a high bluff. Several miles inland on a plateau covered with scrubby pine forests, checkered by small parcels of cleared land, was a log Methodist meetinghouse called the Shiloh Church. Five divisions of Grant's forces set up camp on this plateau, another reserve division commanded by General Lew Wallace was stationed at Crump's Landing a

The Pendulum of War

dozen miles north and Grant set up his own headquarters at the town of Savannah across the river where he planned to wait for Buell's army which would be arriving from the east.

Daily Grant went down the river to inspect the troops on the plateau, then returned at dusk to Savannah to wait for Buell. When General Smith was taken ill with an infection that eventually proved fatal, Grant's old school friend, William T. Sherman, took over Smith's division, which was camped closest to the Shiloh Church.

Many of the men were raw, young volunteers and there were the usual complaints about the rough diet of pork and hardtack and the constant diarrhea which was jokingly referred to as the "Tennessee quickstep," but in general morale was high. In the evenings the young men sat around their campfires swapping stories and listening to calliope music furnished by the steamboats anchored below the bluff.

The Confederates were well aware of their position and there were occasional skirmishes between scouting parties, minor actions that increased noticeably after the first of April. On April 4, while returning from inspecting an outpost, Grant's horse slipped and fell on him, injuring his ankle so severely that his boot had to be cut off and the next day he was hobbling on crutches. On April 5, Sherman noticed an unusual number of rabbits and deer fleeing out of the forest but dismissed it as a natural result of the skirmishing and that night Grant took his headquarter's boat, the *Tigress,* back to Savannah where Buell was expected in the morning.

On the morning of April 6, Grant was drinking coffee at the kitchen table in his headquarters, when he heard the sound of heavy artillery fire from the direction of Pittsburg Landing. While Grant had been assembling his troops at Shiloh, the Confederate commanders had been perfecting a plan of their own. Their forces still outnumbered Grant's divisions, and they had decided to attack him at Shiloh before he could receive reinforcements. Because of the heavy rains, they were delayed in getting underway, but by the night of April 5, they had their troops close enough to the Union camp that they could hear the distant music of the calliopes. At 6:30 A.M. the following morning they launched their attack.

Within fifteen minutes after hearing the cannon, Grant was aboard the *Tigress.* Leaving word for Buell and his forces to join him once they arrived, he crossed the river to Crump's Landing and ordered Wallace to move south by the river road, then hurried on down the river. Just two and a half hours after the battle had begun, Grant reached Pittsburg Landing. As the Confederates had come over in successive waves, many of the raw volunteers had broken in panic and fled to the rear. When Grant came ashore, several thousand of these troops were cowering under the cliffs, refusing to go back into battle. But up on the bluff a pall of black smoke stretched for almost two miles and the sound of heavy firing showed that the main body of the soldiers were now holding their own.

Mounting his horse, Grant rode out to check on the action. Sherman's position at Shiloh had borne the brunt of the attack, though fighting was going on for the entire length of the line. The majority of the troops on both sides were new recruits, but the battle of Shiloh was to be one of the bloodiest of the war. Within an hour of the first charge almost every soldier was in combat with companies separated or overrunning each other as they became scattered through the forest and clearings. The hottest spot was a thicket area east of the Shiloh Church, called the Hornet's Nest. Here Confederate General Johnston was killed and an entire Union division captured. Nightfall brought a welcome lull due to the exhaustion on both sides.

Throughout the day, Grant made repeated tours to the different divisions, an air of coolness about him that bolstered the soldiers' spirits wherever he appeared. At dusk he withdrew to Pittsburg Landing. By now Buell had reached Savannah and come down the river. A legend which grew up around this meeting claims that Buell, appalled by the Union losses, asked Grant what he intended to do since he only had boats enough to get ten thousand men back across the river. Whereupon Grant was supposed to have replied, "By the time I order retreat, that's all the boats I'll need." Actually, the story had no basis in truth. The Union losses had been severe, but the line was holding and at no time had Grant given any sign that he was even considering retreat.

Temporarily, he sought shelter in the log building at the landing, but it was being used as a medical station and the moans of the wounded drove him outside to a large tree. Here Sherman found him, his back against the trunk and his crippled leg stretched out in front of him, the rain dripping from his hatbrim threatening to put out his cigar.

"We've had the devil's own day, haven't we?" Sherman summed up the situation.

"Yes," Grant admitted gruffly, then puffed furiously at the cigar. "Lick 'em tomorrow though."

His prediction was correct. By morning Wallace, who had been delayed by taking the wrong road, arrived with his division and the first of Buell's men began unloading from boats coming down the river. At dawn the action was renewed, but by two in the afternoon the Confederates were being pushed back and by four o'clock they were in full retreat. Grant's forces were too exhausted to pursue them.

The next day the heartbreaking task of burying the dead began. Some of the clearings were so strewn with the fallen that in Grant's own words, "it would have been possible to walk across . . . in any direction, stepping on dead bodies, without a foot touching the ground."

Both the North and South were stunned by the news of the battle of Shiloh. The terrible casualties robbed the victory of any glory. In dead, wounded and missing, the Union had lost thirteen thousand men, the Confederates ten thousand. Two months before, Grant had been the hero of the hour. Now the pendulum swung in the other direction and he was vilified in the papers and called a butcher. In justification of their cowardice, many of the volunteers who had fled the battlefield bombarded their hometown papers with stories of Grant's mismanagement. He was accused of allowing his entire army to become demoralized, of having been drunk in his headquarters when the fighting began, of being totally incompetent. Many newspapers printed what was purported to be the favorite saying among the soldiers: "If you hit Rawlins on the head, you'll knock out Grant's brains."

Grant refused to reply to these stories just as he had refused to reply to the rumors about his leaving the army. Among those who came to his defense, the most active was Sherman, who wrote numerous letters trying to set the facts straight. But Grant's most telling support came when a newspaperman approached Lincoln with a demand that Grant be discharged. "I can't spare this man Grant," the President replied. "He fights."

Four days after the battle, Halleck arrived at Shiloh to take personal command and resume the march on Corinth. Halleck made certain there would be no failure. They remained at Shiloh, adding reinforcements until the army numbered 120,000 men. On April 30, this huge juggernaut slowly started south. Sometimes they covered less than a mile a day and at each stop the entire camp was entrenched and defenses set up as though they expected an attack by a force double their size. In all, the twenty-mile march to Corinth was to take them a month.

It was a time of misery for Grant. Halleck had elevated him to second in command but turned the Army of the Tennessee over to another commander. Grant found himself in the position of a second fiddle with no strings. With nothing to do he grew restless and moody. The outcry over Shiloh was dying down, but Grant had been more deeply hurt by the stories than he let on. As always with idleness, his thoughts turned to Julia and the children. By now she had moved first to St. Louis, then on to Cairo to be near him. One night Sherman found Grant in his tent with most of his possessions already packed. Convinced that his usefulness to the army was over, Grant was preparing to ask for a month's leave to return to his family, after which if he returned to the army at all he planned to ask for a new assignment. Sherman spent several hours, alternately joking with him and in moments of seriousness trying to convince him of the foolhardiness of the move. To Sherman's relief, when he finally left, Grant was unpacking again.

Chapter VIII

Hero of Vicksburg

Until the battle of Shiloh Grant had clung to the stubborn hope that the South would sue for peace. The determination of the Confederate commanders in seizing the initiative at Shiloh changed his opinion. He was convinced now that the South would never give up until their capacity to make war had been completely destroyed, a change in thinking that only added to his conviction that the seizure of the waterways of the Mississippi River would be the means by which the Southern states would be separated and rendered incapable of assisting each other.

On May 29, Halleck's ponderous Union force reached the outskirts of Corinth where once again they entrenched themselves. Throughout the night they could hear trains moving in and out of Corinth to the accompaniment of cheering, as though the Confederates were receiving reinforcements. Halleck issued orders to expect an attack before dawn. Former railroad workers among the soldiers felt differently. Putting their ears to the ground, they insisted that they could tell by the rumble of the cars that the trains were coming in empty and going out full.

The railroad men were correct. The next day when they

Hero of Vicksburg

marched into Corinth, they found the enemy gone. Aware he could not fight a force the size of that commanded by Halleck, General Beauregard had used the delay to get his men and supplies out of the city, instructing the soldiers to cheer throughout the night to give the impression they were greeting new arrivals.

If Grant had been in low spirits during the slow march, the weeks following the capture of Corinth were even more depressing. He felt that Halleck had the troops assembled to push South and deal the enemy a mortal blow, but the War Department was committed to caution. The huge army was broken up. Buell was sent to Chattanooga, Grant went to Memphis and Halleck remained at Corinth.

The summer of 1862 was a time of discouragement for the North as they lost the offensive on all fronts. In the East, McClellan and the Army of the Potomac had failed in their march into Virginia and General Lee had assumed the offensive and was moving into Maryland. In the West, the Confederates replaced Beauregard with the more aggressive General Braxton Bragg. Taking advantage of the division of Halleck's forces, Bragg aimed his strength against Buell's Army of the Ohio, pushing him back across Tennessee all the way into Kentucky. On July 11, when Halleck was called to Washington to replace McClellan as commander in chief so that McClellan could devote full time to the Army of the Potomac, the strength in the West was diluted even further. Grant was restored to command of the Army of the Tennessee at Corinth, but there was no longer a single unified leader in the West and each general worked independently.

When Grant took command at Corinth, his force numbered nine divisions, but by August some of these divisions had to be diverted east to assist Buell. Taking advantage of this weakening of the strength at Corinth, Confederate General Sterling Price seized Iuka, twenty miles distant. Union troops commanded by General William S. (Rosey) Rosecrans drove him out but failed to press their advantage. In October, reinforced by the arrival of General Earl Van Dorn, Price attempted another attack on Corinth itself. Again Rosecrans drove the Confederates back and again failed to pursue. Since the days when he had been considered one of the most brilliant cadets at West Point, Rosecrans had been admired by Grant. When Rosecrans was sent to relieve Buell as commander of the Army of the Ohio, Grant was spared the embarrassment of having to replace him. Crusty, bluff-speaking Rosecrans was much like Grant, serving better when he had complete charge than under orders. Soon he had stopped Bragg's advance and was pushing him back across Tennessee.

At Corinth, Grant was far from idle. Now that his troops were in Confederate territory there were new duties relative to occupation. A major problem was the cotton crop on the captured plantations, which Grant arranged to have harvested and shipped north. Another problem was the number of former slaves pouring into his army headquarters. They had to be fed and put to work. In spite of these occupation duties, Grant remained convinced that if the Union offensive was to get moving again, he was in the position to start it.

That April while Halleck had been moving toward Corinth, Rear Admiral David G. Farragut had taken New Orleans and shortly afterward proceeded upstream as far as Baton Rouge. With the mouth of the Mississippi in Union hands and Union control extending as far south as Memphis, the key point in securing the remaining section of the river was Vicksburg, Mississippi, two hundred miles south of Memphis, heavily fortified and under the command of Confederate General John C. Pemberton.

Despite their personal differences, Grant and Halleck were united in their belief that control of the Mississippi River was essential to victory and by the first of November Grant had

Halleck's permission to move on Vicksburg. The plan was for Grant to move south from Corinth by way of the Mississippi Central Railroad to the capital at Jackson, due east of Vicksburg, from which he would launch the major attack from the east, while Sherman, moving down river, would attack the city from the north at the Chickasaw Bluffs.

It was an able plan, but by its very logic completely obvious to the Confederates. As Grant moved south along the railroad, his supply lines stretched thinner and it was necessary to leave guards along the rail line. Choosing Holly Springs for his main supply depot and leaving what he believed to be a sufficient guard, Grant had reached the town of Oxford by mid-November.

Several days later, while enjoying a visit from Julia and their youngest son, Jesse, Grant received stunning news. During the night the Confederate forces of Van Dorn had swept down on Holly Springs and burned the entire depot to the ground. The loss of his supplies was a devastating blow to Grant's campaign. In only one small and personal matter had Van Dorn's attack failed. Learning that Mrs. Grant was traveling south to see her husband, his men had surrounded the house where she had stopped overnight hoping to take her prisoner. Fortunately Julia had slipped out of town only hours before.

Nothing could be done immediately to offset the loss. Sherman, who was already on his way down the river, launched his attack at Chickasaw Bluffs on December 29, but was forced back with heavy casualties. Joined by McClernand with a division of new Illinois volunteers, they made several minor sorties into Arkansas, then set up camp at Young's Point several miles above Vicksburg on the west side of the river, where Grant joined them in late January 1863.

That winter was another one of discouragement for the North. McClellan was removed from command of the Army of the Potomac and optimistically replaced by General Ambrose Burnside, who suffered another crushing Union defeat at Fredericksburg on December 13. Meanwhile, at Vicksburg, Grant faced the seemingly insurmountable task of getting his campaign under way again. The city stood atop two-hundred-foot bluffs on the east side of the river where its batteries had almost absolute control over all river traffic. Directly across from Vicksburg the river made a long horseshoe bend, with the strip of land inside the bend pointing like a narrow finger directly at the city. It was here at the base of this finger, just out of range of the Vicksburg batteries, that the Union forces were camped. Attack from the river was impossible and Sherman's earlier defeat had demonstrated the infeasibility of attack from the north. Heavy rains, flooding and terrain that had melted into a morass of mud delayed action in any direction.

Once again rumors circulated in the newspapers of Grant's incompetence and drunkenness. The rumors of his drinking reached such proportions that Lincoln summoned one of Grant's former officers, General John Thayer, to question him personally on the matter. When Thayer reported that Grant drank occasionally with his officers, but that he had never seen him take a drink in time of decision or under the stress of battle, Lincoln appeared satisfied. "What I want is generals who will fight battles and win victories. Grant has done this and I propose to stand by him. . . . Ever since he sent that message to Buckner, 'no terms but unconditional surrender,' I have felt that he was the man that I could tie to, though I have never seen him." After that, no move was made to replace Grant.

Bogged down by high water, there was little Grant could do that winter. Unsuccessful attempts were made to dig a canal across the horseshoe and to get gunboats up the neighboring Yazoo River and through the swamps and bayous around Lake Providence on the west. From the beginning, Grant had little confidence in these schemes, but they helped to keep the men occupied and by spring he had come up with a plan of his own, so daring that he kept it secret even from his staff until he had it perfected.

From his new Union headquarters down the river at New Orleans, General Nathaniel P. Banks was planning to move north against Port Hudson, Louisiana, about 150 miles south of Vicksburg. Timing his move to coincide with Banks', Grant intended to march his army down the west side of the river and attempt to run enough gunboats and transports past the batteries to move his men across the river below the city. Here, with a new supply route opened up via Port Hudson and New Orleans, he would swing north to surround Vicksburg from the landward side as he had done at Fort Donelson.

Admiral David D. Porter, in command of the Union gunboats, was enthusiastic. He immediately set men to reinforcing the boats, securing coal barges which they would tow with them and building barriers of hay and cotton bales on the open decks of the transports to keep their boiler fires from being spotted at night. When the plan was presented to Grant's generals, some were dubious at first, but in time all were infected with Grant's self-confidence.

The action began on the night of April 16, when five gunboats and three transports, a number of them towing coal barges, started downstream. Porter led the way in his flagship, followed by three gunboats, the three transports, then the last gunboat. They cast off at one-minute intervals and moved in a course slightly offset from each other so that, if any vessel was sunk, the one behind could continue without stopping.

Grant watched the action from the deck of his flagship anchored upstream. With him were Julia and the children. Once he was on his way, they would return to St. Louis, with the exception of Fred, who was to accompany his father on the campaign. His small figure would become a familiar sight, swashbuckling about camp with Grant's seldom-used dress sword dragging at his side.

All watched anxiously as the boats slipped away. As they came opposite the cliffs, the shore batteries opened fire. Minutes later the banks were ablaze with bonfires set to give the Confederates a better sight of their targets. Equal to this surprise, Porter directed his flagship closer to the bluffs, where return fire was impossible but where the batteries would be forced to deflect at an awkward angle. All the ships were struck, but only one transport was sunk with a direct hit in its boilers. As the rest slipped on down the river, the first move had been a success.

Grant had already started his army down the west bank of the river in two sections commanded by General McClernand and youthful General James B. McPherson. Meanwhile, Sherman made a feint at the Chickasaw Bluffs with another division in an effort to draw Pemberton's attention. Pemberton took the bait and by the time he realized that he was not facing the main body of the army, Grant was twenty-five miles down the river, where he transported his men to the other side and seized the Confederate garrisons at both Grand Gulf and Fort Gibson.

Grant ran into temporary difficulties when he learned that Banks had not yet made his move on Port Hudson. Without Port Hudson in Union hands so that he could receive supplies by way of New Orleans, Grant was now cut off from his supplies. From his scouts, Grant learned that Pemberton had about forty thousand men at Vicksburg, while General Joseph Johnston had an unknown number of men at Jackson due east. Grant's whole strategy must now depend on striking swiftly before these two armies could join. Remembering how Winfield Scott had thrown caution to the winds in the battle for Mexico City and cut himself off from his supplies, Grant decided to do the same. Ordering his soldiers to fill their haversacks with as much food as they could carry, after which they would live off the land, Grant swung his army northeast to meet Johnston first. Soon the great body of moving men was being trailed by farm wagons, carts and light buggies loaded with hams, vegetables and other foodstuffs seized from plantations along the route. Before starting out, Grant sent a message to Halleck, telling him of his plans. He knew that the cautious Halleck would be horror-stricken, but if he had cut himself off from his supplies, Grant had also cut himself off from direct communication. By the time the message could be carried upriver to Cairo and wired to Washington, D.C., and the reply could be sent back along the same slow route, Grant hoped to have won his first victory.

General Johnston marshaled his forces for a fight west of Jackson, but Grant pushed him back and by May 15 had taken the Mississippi capital. Staying only long enough to order the destruction of all factories and rail lines that could aid the enemy, Grant swung west toward Vicksburg. Again he was hampered by the number of former slaves pouring into the camp. On January 1, 1863, Lincoln had issued the initial Emancipation Proclamation freeing the slaves of the states in rebellion as "a fit and necessary war measure." Grant set some of the slaves to work on abandoned plantations, but others were allowed to volunteer for service and moved with his troops toward Vicksburg.

Grant's swift moves had put Pemberton in an untenable position. Johnston wired him to send support at the same time that President Jefferson Davis wired him to hold Vicksburg. Pemberton tried to do a little of each by venturing out from the city to try to stop Grant at Champion Hill and again at Black River, but Grant forced him back. By May 19 he had Vicksburg surrounded and his own supply lines reopened to the north by way of the Yazoo River. After two unsuccessful attempts to storm Vicksburg, Grant settled down for a siege. His lines stretched for fifteen miles, the trenches reinforced with sandbags arranged to leave openings for muskets, then heavy logs on top so that the men could walk about erect. In no place were the trenches more than six hundred yards from the enemy and in some places so close that the Yanks and Rebs exchanged good-natured kidding between their front lines. Army engineers dug underground tunnels beneath the Confederate trenches and blew up several emplacements, but mostly it was a waiting game.

In the East, Lee was marching from a victory at Chancellorsville to meet General George C. Meade, the new commander of the Army of the Potomac, at Gettysburg. The attention of most of the nation was focused on this coming battle, but by now the War Department realized the significance of the action at Vicksburg and sent Grant reinforcements, bringing his force to 75,000 men. Unable to fight his way out against such odds, Pemberton surrendered Vicksburg on July 4, 1863, after a siege of forty-seven days. Once the news reached Port Hudson, it surrendered also, and the length of the Mississippi River was in Union hands. Grant took thirty thousand prisoners at Vicksburg, but instead of shipping them north to prison camps, he instituted a new policy of having them sign paroles that they would not bear arms again and sent them home. The measure brought some criticism, but eventually was approved by the War Department as a wise economy move.

In the newspapers, the Victory of Vicksburg was eclipsed by the Union victory at Gettysburg, which had taken place nearly at the same time. These two great victories, marked the turning point of the war in favor of the North, but the struggle was far from over. While he still commanded a major striking force, Grant hoped to march south into Alabama against Mobile, but bolstered by the Gettysburg victory, the War Department was concentrating its attention on the Army of the Potomac again and a new drive toward Richmond. Those next weeks Grant

Hero of Vicksburg

saw his striking force dissipated as before, with Sherman stationed at Jackson, other troops drawn back to Kentucky and still others sent to reinforce Port Hudson.

Grant was again a public hero. In August he visited Memphis, where he was feted at several banquets. In early September, when he went to New Orleans to confer with Banks, he was entertained again and presented with a large, spirited horse which was only half-broken. Asked to review Banks' troops, Grant galloped down the lines at such a pace that the other officers were spread out in a wild chase behind him. Following the review and another dinner, they started back to town with Grant on the fractious horse galloping out ahead. As the road swung parallel to the railroad track, an engine suddenly came around the corner. The startled horse reared and lost its footing, pining Grant beneath it as it fell.

Carried to the St. Charles Hotel, Grant regained consciousness to find himself almost paralyzed on the right side of his body from the swelling. After a week at the hotel, he was carried by litter aboard a steamboat and returned to Vicksburg. Immediately there was the usual spate of rumors that the accident was the result of drunkenness. Aside from these, Grant's convalescence was not as dreary as expected. Leaving the older children in school in St. Louis, Julia came south to nurse him and they spent a happy month in a spacious mansion overlooking the river.

Then, on October 3, Grant received word of a catastrophic action farther east. On relieving Buell as commander of the Army of the Ohio, General Rosecrans had successfully pushed Braxton Bragg back across Tennessee and reoccupied the key city of Chattanooga only a mile or two from the Georgia border. Believing he had Bragg in full flight, Rosecrans had not allowed his weary men to rest at Chattanooga but had pushed on into Georgia where Bragg, newly reinforced by General James Longstreet, had struck him at Chickamauga Creek.

After two days of fighting, Rosecrans was in full rout. Only the staunch action of the division led by General George Thomas saved his army from complete annihilation as they fled back to Chattanooga, where the Confederates immediately surrounded them. The nearest army of any size that could go to their aid was that of General Burnside at Knoxville, but he, too, had been cut off and was in an equally perilous situation.

Leaving his sickbed, Grant set off for Cairo where he could communicate with the War Department directly by wire. In Cairo he learned the situation was considered too grave for telegraph communication and he was ordered to Louisville, Kentucky, for a secret conference. At a switch point at Indianapolis, the secrecy was lifted when his train was halted so that an important person could board the car. This important person turned out to be Secretary of War Edwin M. Stanton.

The meeting did not get off to an auspicious start. On boarding Grant's train, Stanton went immediately to a bearded and distinguished-looking doctor and wringing the doctor's hand said, "Mr. Grant, I would have recognized you anywhere from your pictures." When Grant's identity as the small, unimpressive-looking man in the rumpled coat had finally been established, they proceeded with their talk.

Stanton brought important news. Grant was being elevated to command of all of the Union army forces west of the Alleghenies with the exception of those commanded by Banks in New Orleans, a position roughly equivalent to the unified command formerly held by Halleck. The promotion had a string to it, however; Grant was also being given the full responsibility for saving Rosecrans besieged forces at Chattanooga.

Chapter IX

Top Command

Grant and Secretary of War Stanton traveled together to Louisville, continuing their talks at Galt House, where it was decided to relieve General Rosecrans and place General George Thomas in command at Chattanooga. It was after dark when the meeting ended and Grant decided to relax by taking a horseback ride before retiring. A large crowd had gathered outside and again one of Grant's more imposing looking aides was temporarily mistaken for the general. According to Bruce Catton, in *Grant Takes Command,* when it was learned that the small man, still walking with a crutch because of his injuries, was U. S. Grant, one disappointed bystander cried, "I thought he was a large man. He would be considered a small chance of a fighter if he lived in Kentucky."

If the evening ride helped refresh Grant's mind for the new responsibilities he faced, he was to have little sleep that night. On his return to Galt House, he was summoned to another meeting with Stanton. According to a report just received from Assistant Secretary of War Charles Dana, who was with the Union troops, Chattanooga was about to surrender. Grant sent an immediate dispatch to Thomas asking an exact accounting of his remaining supplies and ordering him to hold the city at all hazards. Thomas whipped back a reply saying the food on hand was enough to last five or six days and concluding with the words: "I will hold the town until we starve." The public was delighted by this cocky reply, but to Grant it was a sobering appraisal of the seriousness of the situation and he took off immediately to assume personal command.

En route he was delayed briefly at Nashville for a flowery speech by Andrew Johnson, the military governor of Tennessee. A second stop to confer with Rosecrans, who was on his way north after being relieved, was more to Grant's liking. Grant learned that at no time had Rosecrans considered surrendering Chattanooga and had left the troops already working on a plan by which they hoped to extricate themselves. On October 21, Grant reached Bridgeport, Alabama, an important rail junction which had been the main supply depot for Chattanooga before it had been sealed off by the Confederates.

As a result of his conference with Rosecrans, Grant now had a complete picture of the situation at Chattanooga. The Tennessee River on its way to flow eventually into the Ohio made two great sweeps north and south across the state of Tennessee. Rising in the mountains to the northeast, the river flowed south past Knoxville to Chattanooga just above the Georgia border, where it swung west in a series of horseshoe loops, the longest of which reached down to Bridgeport just across the Alabama border, then turned to flow north back across Tennessee to Kentucky. Chattanooga, located where the river swung west, was surrounded on three sides by the Confederates. Directly to the east, Bragg had his emplacements atop the hills at Missionary Ridge. To the south where the river bent to the west, he commanded Lookout Mountain, and farther west, where supplies normally came in from Bridgeport, he had seized the crossing at Brown's Ferry. The closure of the river at this bend below Chattanooga was also cutting off supplies from General Burnside farther up the river at Knoxville. The only way into Chattanooga was through the mountains to the north over a sixty-mile, circuitous trail converted to a morass of mud at this season of the year.

Wasting little time in Bridgeport, Grant took off the next morning over this mountain road. The trip required two days and the way was littered with the carcasses of pack animals that had perished in a vain attempt to get supplies through to the besieged city. In the muddy going, Grant's horse fell on him again and he had to be carried several times while someone else led his horse, but on October 24, Assistant Secretary Dana dispatched a heartening wire to Washington: "Grant arrived last night, wet, dirty and well."

The latter was particularly true. Within a few days Grant wrote Julia that the ride over the mountains seemed to have completely cured his leg injury. Without waiting to change out of his muddy clothes, Grant sat down by the fire in Thomas' headquarters on the night of his arrival and called his first conference. The situation in relation to supplies was grave. The soldiers were reduced to a diet of one small piece of hardtack and an even more miserly cube of salt pork at each meal and guards had been posted at the feed troughs so that hungry men would not try to steal the corn being fed to the animals. But Grant was taken with the plan already worked out by Brigadier General William Farrer Smith, chief engineer of the Army of the Cumberland.

The following morning Grant rode out with Smith to inspect the progress that had been made. At the edge of the river, Smith had salvaged an old engine which he had put to work running a small sawmill. With wood from this mill he was already constructing pontoon bridges. Smith's plan was to march soldiers down their side of the river, slip the pontoons past the outposts at the base of Lookout Mountain under the cover of darkness and seize Brown's Ferry to reopen the supply lines to Bridgeport.

East of the city the picket lines between the Union and the Confederate forces at the base of Missionary Ridge were so close that the men had adopted a kind of good-natured truce, passing jokes across the small strip of no-man's-land that separated them. As Grant rode along the perimeter, he could see the gray uniforms of the Rebs as they moved about their outposts only a short distance away.

Grant returned from the reconnaissance weary but confident in Smith's plan and ordered more soldiers to the building of the pontoons. On October 26, Grant took another ride along the eastern perimeter. At one place he left the others and rode down to the bank of a small stream where he dismounted to get a drink. The commander of the Union picket post recognized the visitor and cried "Turn out the guard," with his men hastily scrambling into line.

Across the creek the Confederate commander, not to be outdone, gave the same cry. Immediately a line of gray uniforms appeared on the opposite bank as the Rebels presented arms also. When Grant had finished his drink, he waved his old slouch hat to them in recognition of their courtesy.

But this exchange of pleasantries did not deter the plan for launching the attack on Brown's Ferry that night. The assault went as planned with the Confederate guard caught by surprise and overpowered and the supply line opened up to Bridgeport again.

The opening of the "cracker line," as the exuberant soldiers dubbed it, brought more than just supplies. By now General Joseph Hooker, with two corps from the Army of the Potomac, was in Bridgeport and Grant was able to tell him to begin moving up. At the same time Sherman, who had inherited Grant's old command of the Army of the Tennessee, was also on his way to assist them.

The attack on Brown's Ferry had taken Bragg by surprise and he sent Longstreet to attempt to regain the position in a night attack. The outnumbered Union defenders lost four hundred men but succeeded in holding the ferry with the help of one of those strange misadventures of battle. With the opening of the attack, a number of frightened teamsters ran for cover. Their abandoned animals, terrified by the noise of the exploding shells, stampeded for the Confederate lines. As they crashed through the forest in the darkness banging their dangling harnesses and wagon braces, the Confederates believed that the Union soldiers had launched a full-scale cavalry charge and withdrew. Following the action the quartermaster in charge of the animals sent Grant a wry recommendation: "I respectfully submit that the mules, for their gallantry in this action, may have conferred upon them the brevet rank of horses." Remembering his own quartermaster's duties in Mexico handling fractious animals, Grant got a hearty laugh.

Even with the supply lines reopened, Grant could not move immediately. Stores were so depleted in Chattanooga that it was November 23 before he was ready to launch the offensive to try to break out of the trap.

The plan of battle was basically simple. Hooker's men were to attack Lookout Mountain on the south. A direct assault on Missionary Ridge was considered suicidal since it was defended by three heavily fortified lines: one at the base of the mountains, another partway up the slopes, and a final line of heavy batteries on the top, but Thomas was to open the attack with a feint at the ridge in an effort to hold Bragg in position. Meanwhile Sherman was to take his troops to the north and climb to the top of the mountain from which position, on a level with the Confederates on top of the ridge, he was expected to make the winning assault.

That first day, while Sherman and Hooker were getting into position, the action was largely confined to Thomas' feint at Missionary Ridge which succeeded in overrunning the Confederate perimeter and securing several miles of territory east of the city. One of the places seized was Orchard Knob, a small hill which Grant used as an observation point the following day. It was a battlefield equaled by few in history, in that from the top of this knoll, Grant was able to take in the entire action of his units. To the south he could see Hooker slowly but victoriously making his way up Lookout Mountain until in midafternoon his men were lost in the mists of what would be called the Battle of the Clouds. Directly ahead he could see Thomas' men, after the action the previous day content with holding their own at the base of the ridge. To the north he could see Sherman working higher and higher to gain the mountain top north of the ridge. By nightfall, it was obvious that Sherman was the one in trouble. His men had gained the top of the mountain only to discover it was not the right one and they were separated by a narrow valley into which they must descend and climb up again to reach Missionary Ridge.

By the third day Hooker was well on his way to victory on Lookout Mountain but Bragg, aware of Sherman's predicament, was diverting troops to the north to pick off Sherman's men as they came up from the valley. To relieve the pressure on Sherman, Grant directed Thomas in another charge at Missionary Ridge itself. From his position on the hill he watched in stunned disbelief as Thomas' men went over the first Confederate emplacement at the bottom of the ridge, surged on up the mountain to the second, then over the top to win the position.

This successful assault on Missionary Ridge led to another legend of the Civil War, that the soldiers had acted without the command of their officers and that the first one over the top had cried, "You know, boys, you're all going to be court-martialed!"

While the success of the assault on the ridge was a surprise to Grant and almost everyone, it was carried out under the orders of the Union officers, who shortly after the charge began had been forced to improvise as they moved. The first charge had taken them over the Confederate line at the base of the ridge, where they discovered they were in the immediate range of the Confederate batteries at the top. Instead of waiting to be cut down by this deadly fire, the officers had ordered the men on, in many places the Union soldiers overtaking the Rebels, who were also fleeing up the slopes, making the fire from their comrades above almost impossible. Once up the slopes, they found that the precipitous terrain and numerous small gullies afforded a new protection so that most of the cannonballs were now shooting harmlessly over their heads. Using this cover, they had continued on to the top.

The victory was so unexpected that soldiers danced, hugged each other and piled astride the captured cannon. The siege was broken and Bragg was fleeing into Georgia. Grant could only follow a short distance, then Sherman's forces had to be pulled away and sent to assist Burnside at Knoxville.

The victory at Chattanooga sent a tidal wave of optimism through the North. Grant had saved the day again. There were no more innuendos in the press about his drinking. Lincoln called on the nation for a national Thanksgiving. Grant was awarded a special gold medal by Congress. The citizens of Illinois presented him with a sword, its hilt set with diamonds and the gold scabbard engraved with the names of all the battles he had won. Newspapers that had been filled with slurs about him only a year before slyly hinted that Grant might be a Presidential candidate in the coming elections of 1864. Grant ended these rumors by telling the Democratic Central Committee of Illinois, who wished to put his name in nomination, that he had no interest aside from winning the war.

From Chattanooga Grant's headquarters were moved to Nashville, where he was able to have Julia join him. In January 1864 he faced a private crisis of his own when Fred, who was now back in school in St. Louis, was stricken with a combination of typhoid and pneumonia. Securing permission from the War Department, Grant rushed to St. Louis where he found that only hours before Fred had passed the crisis and would recover.

In an effort to relieve Grant's tension, friends insisted he accompany them to the theater. When the audience learned that he was there, they demanded that he move forward in the box so that everyone could see him. Returning to his hotel, Grant found another huge crowd and he was asked to step out onto a balcony so that all could see him. Embarrassed by the clamor, Grant used a theatrical trick that he would employ many times after that in order to spare himself from public speaking. He refused to make a speech but instead of withdrawing abruptly while people still wanted to look at him, he fumbled in his pockets, produced one of the long cigars that had become his trademark, slowly prepared it for smoking, lighted it after several unsuccessful tries, then waved it in farewell as he withdrew. For a shy man with little political aplomb it was a masterpiece of showmanship. The people could find plenty of long-winded speakers; it was enough just to watch General Grant light his cigar!

When Fred was well enough to travel, he and Julia joined Grant in Nashville again. Their weeks together were brief. Not long after the victory at Chattanooga, President Lincoln had introduced a measure into Congress reviving the old rank of lieutenant general, a move which shook up the entire military setup. With numerous generals, including Grant, holding the top rank of major general, it has been relatively easy to replace any commander who was unsuccessful with another, thought better fitted for his duties. But it was also a system which had given rise to many petty jealousies, particularly in the case of the Army of the Potomac. Once someone was named to the new rank of lieutenant general, he would irrevocably outrank all below him and there could be no shifting of top command.

Lincoln did not move to fill the new office immediately. Apparently he was waiting to see if Grant had political pretensions. Finally satisfied that Grant had none, Lincoln summoned him to Washington on March 3, to take over the new position as lieutenant general of the Union army.

Accompanied by Fred, Grant arrived in Washington on March 8. A reception had been planned for him at the station, but Grant arrived unnoticed at an earlier hour and took a carriage to the hotel. Dressed in a long linen duster that covered his uniform, he signed the register, "U. S. Grant and son, Galena, Illinois." The harassed clerk directed him to a small room on an upper floor. Grant was already on his way upstairs before he was recognized and hurriedly called back and given a larger suite. Tired from their trip, Grant and Fred washed up and made their way down to the dining room. They had barely started to eat when there was a standing ovation from the surrounding diners. Once again Grant avoided making a speech, but he and Fred hurried back to their room, leaving most of their meal uneaten.

Grant could not avoid the limelight forever. That evening he had to go to the White House to pay his respects to Lincoln. Unlike Stanton, Lincoln recognized him immediately and came forward to shake his hand warmly. They made an incongruous pair, with Lincoln standing six foot four and Grant a scant five foot nine. After being presented to Mrs. Lincoln, Grant was escorted into another room which was even more crowded and where he was asked to stand on a velvet sofa so everyone could see him. Grant obliged but with a reluctance that showed that he was not enjoying the display. Once down from the couch, he quickly made his excuses. The following day he was to return to the White House, where he was to be formally presented with his new rank in the presence of Lincoln and his Cabinet. At the door Lincoln thoughtfully handed Grant a copy of the speech that he intended to make so that Grant could prepare a reply.

Back at the hotel Grant read Lincoln's speech and prepared his own response with Fred's eager assistance. The next day at the White House ceremony he made no effort to reply extemporaneously but unabashedly pulled out a sheet of paper and read his brief acceptance: "Mr. President, I accept the commission with gratitude for the high honor conferred. With the aid of the noble armies that have fought in so many fields for our common country, it will be my earnest endeavor not to disappoint your expectations. I feel the full weight of the responsibilities now devolving on me; and I know that if they are met, it will be due to those armies, and, above all, to that favor of Providence which leads both nations and men."

It had been a long jump from a resigned and discredited infantry captain to top command of all the Union forces, but Grant's feelings of personal triumph were sobered by the terrible responsibility he was assuming. According to the new setup, Halleck would continue to handle the paperwork in Washington as chief of staff, but Grant would give the commands. On only one point was Grant outweighed. Lincoln wished extra troops sent to General Banks in New Orleans so that he could move west against Texas. With Texas cut off from the rest of the South by the Union control of the Mississippi River, Grant personally felt that the few forces operating there had no major bearing on the war. Aside from this, he was given a free hand. Just how free, he learned when Lincoln informed him that even he did not want to know Grant's battle plans for fear he might unintentionally let them leak out.

Discounting the small Confederate units still operating west of the Mississippi and holding various outposts in the deep South, Grant believed that there were only two major Confederate armies to be beaten: the Confederate Army of Tennessee, where General Joseph Johnston had just replaced

Braxton Bragg, and the Army of Northern Virginia, led by General Robert E. Lee. Grant still felt that it would be the Union armies in the West that would win the war, by breaking the South apart and destroying her potential to continue fighting. That is where he longed to be, but he knew psychologically he should go with the Army of Potomac. After three years of fighting and 140,000 casualties, the Army of the Potomac was presently encamped only twenty-five miles from its first battlefield of the war, at Bull Run. Its defeats could not be blamed entirely on leadership. From the beginning it had faced a more formidable opponent in the brilliant General Lee than the western armies had confronted. At the same time that its commanders planned their offensives, they had to remember that the Army of the Potomac was also responsible for the vital defense of the capital at Washington, another problem not faced by the Union armies in the West.

Leaving Washington, Grant journeyed briefly down to Culpeper, Virginia, to talk with General Meade. It was a touchy meeting, for Meade expected to be replaced as head of the Army of the Potomac. Instead, the two men found they had much in common. Leaving Meade in command, Grant returned to Washington feeling encouraged. Here Grant instituted one change with Lincoln's approval. Until now the cavalry had served principally in an auxiliary sense, guarding rail and freight lines and acting as couriers. Grant received permission to create an independent cavalry corps to be used as an aggressive fighting force, with youthful General Philip Sheridan as its commander.

Traveling to Nashville, Grant gave Sherman orders for the continuing campaign in the west, then with Julia and Jesse he returned to Washington, found them a place to live and headed south to join the Army of the Potomac.

He was in full command now, the eyes of the nation on him

and his plans unknown even to Lincoln. As he rode into the camp at Culpeper, a short, slight man in a rumpled uniform and dusty soft hat, he did not look like much of a leader, but all along the line of tents there were expectant whispers: "U. S. Grant is here."

Chapter X

The Final Blow

Though Grant had been pleasantly surprised with the immediate accord that had sprung up between him and General Meade, not all the officers of his new command were as favorable to the change in leadership. The Army of the Potomac was more observant of rules and regulations than the armies in the West and Grant's carelessness of dress was annoying to many of the "spit and polish" generals. Others, remembering Grant as only a mediocre student at West Point, were inclined to credit his past victories to sheer luck.

Even the soldiers greeted Grant with curiosity but reservation. There were no spontaneous cheers when he appeared but more an air of watchful waiting. It was perhaps as well that officers and men did not know that Grant had the same reservation about them. He would have preferred to have been going against Lee supported by his tested generals, Sherman and Thomas, and his ever-dependable Army of the Tennessee, but with a war to be won, it was not a time for making friends.

Grant had already consulted with Sherman and the other generals in the West and he gave orders for two smaller campaigns that were to coincide with his own action. General Franz Sigel was sent to seize the agriculturally rich Shenandoah

Valley, a major source of food supplies for the South, and General Butler was directed down the coast to move up the James River below Richmond.

Grant hoped to get his campaign underway on April 25, which would have been just two days after his forty-second birthday, but last-minute details held him at Culpeper another week. Bowing to custom, he appeared before the men for a final review dressed in full dress uniform, wearing sword and gloves and sitting astride his big bay horse, Cincinnati. They would not see him in full uniform again.

Late on the evening of May 3, 1864, the Union supply trains started moving out from their base at Fredericksburg, south of Washington, with Grant and the troops following early the next morning. Their first objective was the crossing of the Rapidan River, which was accomplished without sign of the enemy.

By noon Grant had made the crossing at Germanna Ford and was seated on the porch of an abandoned farmhouse eating his lunch and watching the lines of soldiers still moving across the pontoon bridge. Directly ahead of them was an area roughly twelve miles square of dense, second-growth timber called the Wilderness. A single road, along which they were traveling, cut through the Wilderness from north to south, but it was intersected by several crossroads running east and west. With Lee and his Army of Northern Virginia situated at Orange to the east, Grant's immediate aim was to get through the Wilderness and around Lee to the south in a flanking movement that would cut him off from Richmond.

While Grant was still eating, a courier galloped up with a Confederate message which had been intercepted and decoded. Lee, with roughly 75,000 men opposed to Grant's ninety thousand, was moving out from Orange to intercept Grant in the Wilderness where the fire power of the Union artillery would be offset by the heavy protection of the forest. Grant could not afford to get too far ahead of his slow-moving supply train which was moving down to the west, but he ordered the march speeded up so that his troops would reach the crossroads ahead of Lee.

That night Grant slept in a headquarters tent close by the farmhouse, but at 5 A.M. the following morning the army was moving south again. Two hours later Lee's forces were spotted coming in along the crossroads and the battle of the Wilderness, which would rank with Shiloh as one of the bloodiest encounters of the entire war, began. In the dense growth companies and whole divisions became separated, with men crashing through the trees, crouching behind stumps, rocks, and deadfalls, and firing at anything ahead that moved. As the enemy broke through in one area, they were pushed back in another with neither side gaining a noticeable advantage throughout the day.

The Army of the Potomac had its first glimpse of Grant's coolness under fire. Early in the morning he had ridden into the Wilderness as far as the first crossroad where he had set up his field headquarters on a small rise. During the fighting, as shells began falling around the headquarters, Grant sent an orderly to lead his horse to shelter behind the hill while he remained on top trying to make out the action through his field glasses. Finally a distraught officer suggested that it might be wise to withdraw to his old headquarters at the Germanna Ford. Grant stared at the officer coldly. "It strikes me it would be better to order up some artillery and defend this location," he said.

Nightfall brought a lull in the fighting, but the woods were filled with the cries and moans of the wounded, some of whom were burned to death by forest fires which had been ignited in the dry growth.

Early the next morning the Confederates launched a heavy assault on the Union right, scattering the troops fighting under General John Sedgwick. An officer who had fought against Lee previously approached Grant in alarm. "General Grant, this is a crisis that cannot be looked upon too seriously. I know Lee's methods well. . . . He will throw his whole army between us and the Rapidan and cut us off completely from our communications."

Grant puffed furiously at his cigar then, removing it, replied, "I am heartily sick of hearing about what Lee is going to do. . . . Go back to your command and try to think of what we are going to do ourselves."

Grant knew what he was going to do. Divisions were shifted and the gap was plugged. When the second night fell, the Union soldiers still held the north and south road, but their losses had been severe.

On the morning of May 7, Lee did not launch another attack and Grant gave orders for his army to prepare to march. Wearily the soldiers obeyed. For those who had fought with the Army of the Potomac before, it seemed a familiar story. They had met Lee; he had inflicted heavy losses, now they were withdrawing to reorganize. It was only when they were assembled on the road, and received orders to continue marching south, that they grasped the truth. Grant's original aim had been to outflank Lee and without stopping to count his losses, which numbered fifteen thousand, that was what he intended to do.

As Grant overtook and passed the long lines of weary marching men, for the first time he was greeted with spontaneous cheers. The Army of the Potomac wasn't pulling back cautiously to lick its wounds. This time they were being led by a general who knew how to fight!

The battle of the Wilderness had been Grant's initial test and he had his soldiers solidly behind him now. Even the citizens of the North were heartened in spite of the heavy losses. Everywhere there was a wave of new optimism. This time they were going to finish the war. It was perhaps just as well that neither the soldiers nor the people knew the real truth yet: that

The Final Blow

the Wilderness was not really a separate engagement but just the opening of one great battle that would last almost a year.

Grant's new objective became Spotsylvania, an important junction of the roads twelve miles to the southeast beyond the Wilderness. Hoping to reach it ahead of Lee, he dispatched a detachment of cavalry which reached the town first; however, the dust clouds raised by his huge supply train lumbering to the west of the Wilderness could not be concealed. Guessing Grant's objective, Lee took off for Spotsylvania by a shorter route. His forces drove back the Union cavalry, and when Grant arrived on May 8, he found Lee's forces entrenched and waiting. An ineffectual assault was attempted against the Confederate lines that afternoon and the following morning the battle began in earnest. It was the story of the Wilderness all over again, only this time the battle was fought on open ground. For two days the fighting continued steadily, both sides making occasional gains in one area only to be driven back in another.

On May 11 there was a brief lull while both sides cared for their wounded and buried their dead. Grant used the respite to report to Halleck on the first six days of fighting, concluding with the words: "I propose to fight it out on this line if it takes all summer." Headlined in the newspapers across the country, the words became almost as famous as his "unconditional surrender" note at Fort Donelson, but they evoked an optimism that would not last.

On May 12 and 13 the fighting was resumed with the Union making what appeared to be conclusive gains. There was another lull followed by more fighting and by May 18 the Union forces had been brought to a standstill again. On May 19, leaving Generals Horatio Wright and Ambrose Burnside at Spotsylvania, Grant ordered the main body of his forces south again in another dogged attempt to get between Lee and Richmond.

Lee refused to be drawn into the open where Grant's superior numbers could be used as an advantage. Fighting in a defensive pattern, he backed slowly south until he had all of his men below the North Anna River where by the end of the month they had set up heavily fortified lines along the Virginia Central Railroad extending south and east to Cold Harbor.

By now Grant had progressed far enough south that his supply base was shifted from Fredericksburg to White House on the Pamunkey River, with supplies coming up the river from the coast. Grant realized that Lee was not going to be tempted into the open but was going to fight the rest of the war from behind heavily defended entrenchments, making the Union forces come to him. Accepting the challenge, Grant hurled his men against Cold Harbor on June 3, 1864. It was one of the worst decisions he ever made and one he would regret the rest of his life. In the space of only a couple of hours he lost seven thousand men with absolutely no gain.

News of Cold Harbor swung the pendulum of public opinion against Grant again. The nickname "the Butcher," which had been hung on him at Shiloh, was revived. As before, Grant appeared to ignore the slanders and concentrated on the job ahead.

It was true that in none of the fighting in the West had Grant faced as clever an enemy as Lee. From the days when his unblemished record that had been help up as an example to the other West Point cadets, through his brilliant service in the Mexican War as Winfield Scott's special protégé, Lee had been building up a psychological advantage over the other generals. His reputation as the "perfect soldier," coupled with the fact that he was in truth a brilliant tactician, made him a doubly formidable opponent. But in Grant, a stubbornly determined adversary unlike any he had faced before, Lee was also getting some surprises. Where many commanders were inclined to confine their attention to a single major battle and be either elated or dismayed by its outcome, Grant's greatness lay in his ability to keep an entire campaign so vividly in his mind that, if set-

The Final Blow

backs were encountered in one area, he could ignore these seeming catastrophes in pursuit of his overall plan.

Thus it was with the slaughter at Cold Harbor. On moving out from Culpeper on May 4, Grant had already instituted a huge plan of operations, including the armies in the West. If he had suffered a setback, this was only incidental to the continuing progress of the entire picture. Barely taking time to recover from his losses, Grant ordered his army south again, with the important rail junction city of Petersburg as his next objective.

Believing that the victory at Cold Harbor had thrown Grant into a position where he could only fritter away the strength of his army on continued, futile assaults, Lee was briefly fooled. When reports reached him that the Union army was again marching south, he discounted them as another diversionary move to lure him into the open. It was not until mid-June, when Grant had bypassed Richmond and had his troops safely across the James River that Lee realized his plan and began falling back as hastily as possible.

Like Richmond, Petersburg was heavily fortified. The advance divisions of Grant's army managed to force their way through the outer defenses but failed to follow this advantage. By the time Grant arrived with the main portion of his army, Lee was there ahead of him and waiting again. The Union forces attempted to storm the entrenchments, but after heavy casualties, Grant settled down for a siege.

For his headquarters, Grant chose City Point at the Y-shaped junction of the Appomattox and James Rivers. Here he could receive supplies and men coming up the James River from the coast and direct them northwest up the James River toward Richmond or southwest along the Appomattox toward Petersburg. Grant immediately ordered the bringing up of heavy artillery and digging of entrenchments in a curving half-moon line that closed off both cities to the east.

Before the end of June one final attempt was made to break the Confederate line. A number of Pennsylvania soldiers dug a mine beneath one of the Confederate forts and blew it up with a tremendous explosion. But as Union soldiers charged into the gaping crater, they found themselves the helpless victims of Confederate gunfire from the rim and were forced back after suffering almost as many casualties as the Confederates had lost in the initial explosion.

Since Grant had marched south, public sentiment in the North had been on an emotional seesaw: jubilation as the army continued on after the Wilderness to Spotsylvania, horror at the slaughter at Cold Harbor, and now bitter disappointment when it was learned that, in spite of the fact that Grant had driven Lee back to Petersburg and Richmond, he had not forced a decisive victory. Adding to the gloom that settled over the North that summer was the fact that the war in the West also seemed to be going poorly. Before Grant had gotten under way from Culpeper, Nathaniel Banks had failed in his expedition up the Red River toward Texas. General Butler had not succeeded in his move up the James River. Sigel's efforts in the Shenandoah Valley had come to nothing, as well as those of General David Hunter, who had been sent to replace him. Even Sherman, though moving slowly south through Georgia, had yet to come to real grips with the Confederate forces of General Johnston, now holed up behind heavy fortifications at Atlanta.

It was an election year and the Northern Democrats were talking peace and putting up George B. McClellan as their candidate. Lincoln would be the Republican candidate again, but his chances for reelection seemed to be fading with each new report from the front. In July a wave of panic was added to the general gloom when General Jubal Early, who had been sent into the Shenandoah Valley by Lee, moved briefly north, threatening Washington itself and burning Chambersburg,

The Final Blow

Pennsylvania, in retaliation for the damage done in Shenandoah. There were frantic pleas in the newspapers for Grant to give up his foolhardy campaign and bring the Army of the Potomac back to defend the capital.

Only Grant seemed unperturbed. He hurried north to study the situation personally and put the aggressive Phil Sheridan in command of a new campaign in the Shenandoah Valley, then returned to City Point. According to their agreement, Grant had not revealed his campaign plan to Lincoln, but when he reached Petersburg, the President had wired him that the overall strategy was finally becoming clear. However, during those frightening, depressing months of the summer of 1864, few others in the North saw the plan, only the terrible weariness of the war and the steadily mounting casualty lists. While waiting at City Point for the rest of the war to take shape, Grant was not idle. He attempted no major assaults on the Confederate lines, but slowly extended his own lines so that they began to curl around Petersburg and Richmond like giant tongs, forcing Lee to spread his defenses thinner and thinner.

Then in late summer of 1864 all of Grant's plan began to fall together like the pieces of a giant jigsaw puzzle. Sherman reached Atlanta and, with the city under siege, President Jefferson Davis hastily replaced General Johnston with General John B. Hood. The move was ineffectual and on September 2, Atlanta fell to Sherman. A week later Admiral Farragut seized Mobile Bay. By the end of the month, Sheridan had won his first victory over Jubal Early in the Shenandoah Valley. On abandoning Atlanta instead of trying to halt Sherman, General Hood decided on a foolish countermove of his own back to the north toward Tennessee. Sherman split his forces and sent part of his army under General Thomas north to fight Hood, while he set fire to Atlanta and with the rest started marching east across Georgia to the sea.

By mid-December news had arrived of Thomas' decisive victories over Hood at Franklin and Nashville, Tennessee, putting the Confederate army of the West out of the war as an effective fighting unit. A week later Sherman reached Savannah on the coast and without stopping started north through the Carolinas to joint Grant. Hood was replaced by Johnston again for the Confederates, but by now his fighting force was so depleted he could not oppose Sherman with much more than guerrilla action. By early 1865 Sheridan had successfully defeated Jubal Early at Waynesboro and Charlottesville, concluding his Shenandoah Valley campaign.

From gloom the North swung back to optimism again. The news of the fall of Atlanta and Mobile had been enough to turn the elections and on November 8, 1864, Lincoln was reelected by a popular majority of over 400,000 votes.

From a tent encampment on the bluffs above the junction of the rivers, City Point had grown into a sizable town with numerous wooden buildings. Through the long campaign the ever-dependable Rawlins had served as Grant's secretary, valet, adviser, confidant and self-appointed guardian, but that winter Julia came south to be with Grant, living in a hastily constructed addition behind his headquarters and eating at his officers' mess. There were numerous important visitors, including Lincoln, who arrived in March and remained for three weeks, living aboard the steamer *River Queen*.

By March 23 Sherman was at Greensboro, North Carolina, only 120 miles to the south. Leaving his troops, he came north to talk with Grant. In a meeting with the two generals, Lincoln outlined his plans for the peace. Lincoln liked the terms Grant had given Pemberton at Vicksburg. The President wanted no reprisals, only the written promise of the Confederate commanders that they would not bear arms again so that they could return to their homes and begin the task of rebuilding the South.

The Final Blow

With the extension of Grant's lines and Sherman closing in from the south, Lee's position daily was growing more desperate. Once Sherman arrived, he would be surrounded, making defeat inevitable. His only hope of escape was a corridor of land still open to the west by which he might reach Lynchburg and possibly join there with the remnants of Johnston's forces. With this in mind, early in March Lee launched an attack on Fort Stedman on the Union line. His troops were successful in overrunning the fort, but more Union troops were rushed in and Lee was contained again. It was to be his last offensive move of the war.

On March 29, after leaving a conference with Lincoln, Grant sent orders for Sheridan's cavalry, reinforced by one infantry division, to attack the Confederate flanks southwest of Petersburg. His orders stated: "I feel now like ending the matter if it is possible to do so...."

It was possible and the end came swiftly. For three days fierce fighting ranged along a short front from the Dinwiddie Courthouse to the area called Five Points, but by April 1 Sheridan had broken through Lee's right flank. On receiving this news, Grant issued orders for a fresh assault along the full length of his siege lines. In some places the Confederates held and inflicted heavy casualties, but in others the Union soldiers broke through and by April 5, Petersburg was evacuated and Lee was fleeing west southwest. Ordering Sheridan and Meade to cut him off, Grant rode into Petersburg just long enough to set up new headquarters there, then headed southwest himself in order to keep up with the action. En route he learned that Richmond had fallen also.

On the night of April 5, Grant was in camp along the Southside Railroad when there was a commotion outside his tent. A Confederate soldier had been captured and was demanding to see the general. Grant recognized the man as a spy, who was carrying a message from Sheridan rolled in a piece of foil inside his mouth. According to the dispatch Sheridan had successfully taken Jetersville, cutting Lee off from escape toward the south, and Lee's forces were now camped only a short distance to the north at Amelia Courthouse.

Though it was late, Grant decided to join Sheridan at once. The camp lay sixteen miles away across a wooded no-man's-land not claimed by either force. Accompanied by four aides and a guard of fourteen men, Grant started off through the forest. He passed so close to several Confederate outposts that he could see the pickets moving about their fires through the trees. Grant's appearance at Sheridan's camp came as a surprise to everyone. After a hasty conference, Grant continued on to Meade's nearby headquarters.

At dawn it became evident that Lee had left Amelia Courthouse and was hurrying west toward Farmville where there were bridges that would take him north of the Appomattox River and on toward Appomattox Station where he would be able to receive supplies from Lynchburg.

Grant sent Sheridan in pursuit and there was heavy fighting along Lee's flank throughout the day, but Lee reached Farmville first and moved his weary men across the river, burning the bridges behind him.

Grant rode into Farmville on April 7 to find his quarry gone again, but the Union soldiers had managed to save one bridge from destruction. That evening Grant sat on the porch of the hotel watching the long lines of soldiers march by and on toward the remaining bridge. Other soldiers had started small bonfires in the streets and some filed past the hotel carrying firebrands and singing "John Brown's Body." Stepping to the edge of the porch, Grant watched them with a strange sadness in his eyes. It had been a long, bloody road since John Brown's ill-fated attack on Harpers Ferry in 1859.

Retiring into the hotel, he composed a note to Lee:

The Final Blow

> The results of the last week must convince you of the hopelessness of further resistance on the part of the Army of Northern Virginia in this struggle. I feel that it is so, and regard it as my duty to shift from myself the responsibility of any further effusion of blood by asking of you the surrender of that portion of the Confederate States army known as the Army of Northern Virginia.

It was after midnight and Grant had to be awakened when a courier arrived with Lee's reply. In it Lee refused to admit that his situation was hopeless but left the way open for further communication. Early the next morning Grant crossed the river so he could keep in contact with Lee. Several more notes were exchanged and another day passed with no agreement. By April 9 Lee had reached Appomattox Courthouse, but Union forces had gotten around him, cutting him off from reaching Appomattox Station. Demoralization was sweeping his troops. Many soldiers were stacking their arms and taking off through the trees for home. Other units remained with him but without arms. Almost all were hungry. Lee sent another note to Grant, accepting his proposal for a meeting. Grant ordered his forces to cease firing and raise truce flags all along the lines, while one of his aides, Colonel Orville Babcock, was dispatched to escort Lee to a meeting place for his choice. The final blow had been struck.

Chapter XI

"Let Us Have Peace"

The meeting between Grant and Lee was arranged for April 9, Palm Sunday, at Wilmer McLean's home, a two-storied brick house with a long veranda across the front. Escorted through the Union lines by Colonel Babcock, Lee arrived first, accompanied only by an aide, Colonel Charles Marshall. The Confederate general looked every inch the great commander, wearing full dress uniform complete with sash and jeweled sword.

His appearance was in marked contrast to that of Grant, who rode up a short time later, accompanied by Rawlins, Sheridan, Assistant Adjutant General T. S. Bowers and several other staff officers. Grant wore an ordinary soldier's coat with his stars hastily tacked to the shoulders, no sword and a battered felt hat. His boots and clothes were so spattered with mud that one of the men present described him as resembling "a fly speck on a side of beef." But Grant meant no discourtesy to Lee by his rough appearance. In his hasty night ride to join Sheridan and Meade at Jetersville, he had left all his clothing behind and his baggage had failed to catch up with him.

Grant entered the house alone to speak to Lee first, the two commanders exchanging a few reminiscences about the Mex-

"Let Us Have Peace"

ican War. Then Grant called in his other officers and they got down to the terms of surrender.

In the previous notes that had passed between them, Grant had explained that he had no powers to make any political commitments but could only accept the surrender of Lee's army on the same terms as had been offered at Vicksburg. Lee agreed and Grant sat down at a small, round-topped table. Puffing furiously on the meerschaum pipe which he had substituted today for his usual cigar, he wrote the terms on the pages of his order book. On the ride to the McLean house Grant had worried about the possibility of having to accept Lee's sword, which he felt would be an embarrassment to both of them. After writing out the provision for the men to give their paroles and turn in their arms to the Union forces, he added a clause that all officers were to retain their sidearms, and tacked on a final sentence: "This done, each officer and man will be allowed to return to his home, not to be disturbed by U. S. authority so long as they observe their paroles and the laws in force where they may reside."

In the North many rabid Republican radicals were already demanding war trials and the hanging or imprisonment of the Confederate leaders. With this final clause Grant ruled out retaliation. If he appeared to be overreaching his military powers, he knew he was acting according to Lincoln's wishes.

Lee accepted the terms, pointing out the omission of one word and the sheet was given to Bowers to be formally written out. In his agitation Bowers made three attempts at the copy, each time making an error. He finally relinquished the task to another of Grant's aides, Colonel Ely S. Parker, a full-blooded Seneca Indian who was as impassive and calm as his commanding general.

While Parker was busy writing, Lee and Grant discussed two other problems. Lee pointed out that his officers, unlike those of the Union army, furnished their own mounts and asked that they be allowed to keep their horses. Having been a farmer, Grant realized the importance of these horses to men returning to their farms. He not only granted Lee's request but ordered that every Confederate soldier who had supplied a horse was to chose one from the pool of captured Confederate animals to take home with him. When Lee also pointed out that his men were without food, Grant ordered that they immediately be supplied with rations.

The terms written out and signed, Lee again left the meeting first, with Grant following to salute from the porch. A few minutes later Grant prepared to return to his own forces. Throughout the meeting Lee's face had remained sad and solemn and Grant, with his usual thoughtfulness, had assumed a matching air of gravity. Inside, his emotions were seething and he was not as cool headed as he appeared. As he was riding away from the McLean house, one of his officers had to inquire if he didn't intend to let the War Department and the rest of the nation know what had happened. With a look of stunned surprise, Grant ordered an immediate halt and, dismounting and seating himself on a rock, he hastily wrote the message for a telegram telling of the surrender.

As couriers spread the news through the Union lines, cannons boomed salutes, bands played and men sang, wept, prayed and danced. Usually sedate General Meade galloped bareheaded along the lines shouting, "It's over, boys! It's all over!"

Once the terms had been signed, Union and Confederate officers who had been classmates at West Point or friends before the war visited each other's camps. Among those who came to see Grant was his old friend General James Longstreet. Remembering how Longstreet had invited him to join a game of cards at their last meeting in St. Louis, Grant sought to put Longstreet at ease by suggesting that they should get together soon to finish that card game. His voice choked with

"Let Us Have Peace"

emotion, Longstreet echoed Grant's own feelings by asking, "Why do men fight who were born to be brothers?"

The fighting was over; but Grant, along with many others, knew that the war would not really be concluded until prisoners had been exchanged, soldiers discharged, accounts settled and arrangements completed for accepting the seceding states back into the Union. Without waiting to take part in the formal surrender ceremonies which were scheduled to take place at Appomattox Courthouse on April 12, Grant set off for City Point, where Julia was waiting. Taking no part in the general jubilation that was going on around him, he spent several hours clearing up paperwork on his desk, then the two of them boarded a steamer for Washington, D.C., arriving early on the morning of April 13.

After a conference with Stanton, Grant met with Lincoln and the other members of his Cabinet at the White House on April 14, where he gave the President his firsthand account of Lee's surrender. As Grant was leaving the meeting, Lincoln asked the general and Julia to be his guests that evening at a performance at the Ford Theater. However, during the course of the meeting, Grant had received a note from Julia saying she was anxious to leave the capital for Burlington, New Jersey, where they had purchased a house and the three older children were now attending school. Explaining the situation, Grant refused the invitation.

Back at the hotel, Grant found Julia upset over an unpleasant incident that had occurred earlier in the hotel dining room. While she was having lunch with Mrs. Rawlins, Jesse and Mrs. Rawlins' young daughter, four men at an adjoining table had stared at them so rudely and made such an obvious attempt to overhear their conversation that the women had been forced to hurry up the two small children and leave the room without finishing their lunch. At the time Grant brushed this aside as only another demonstration of public curiosity about him and his family; but that evening as they were driving to the station in a carriage with its curtains drawn against the cold night air, a horseman galloped past them, then whirled back to brush aside the curtains and stare in at them rudely. At the station they boarded a private car and did not learn until later that another stranger had boarded the train and tried to force his way into their quarters but had been restrained and thrown off the train by the crewmen.

Their route to Burlington required them to leave the train at Philadelphia and cross the Delaware River by ferry where another train would carry them on to Burlington. It was midnight when they reached Philadelphia, but en route to the ferry Grant suggested they stop at a hotel restaurant for something to eat. They had placed their orders when a messenger handed Grant a telegram. Grant's face paled as he read it, then, cautioning Julia to keep her composure, he told her that Lincoln had been shot at Ford's Theater and was not expected to live and he was ordered back to the capital immediately.

After seeing Julia safely to Burlington, Grant was back in Washington by dawn. He found the capital in a turmoil of emotion with wild rumors that the President's assassination was the first step in a Confederate plot to reopen the war. It was later learned that the four men in the hotel dining room, the rider who had pulled backed the carriage curtains and the man on the train had been part of the conspiracy, with Grant marked for assassination also. Charged with the security of the capital, Grant briefly succumbed to the rumors long enough to order the arrest of several former members of the Confederate government, orders which fortunately were never carried out and quickly rescinded once the panic died and it was learned that Lincoln's death was not a Southern plot but the work of the crazed actor John Wilkes Booth and a small handful of associates.

"Let Us Have Peace"

But the damage had been done. Lincoln's plan for an easy peace and reconciliation with the South fell apart with his death. Congress already had many radical members whose hatred for the South was unbending. Had Lincoln lived he might have kept them under control, but Andrew Johnson, the new president, was a violent South hater himself. Though born in the South, as the son of an impoverished Tennessee farmer, Johnson had a long-standing dislike for the elite, upperclass Southerners. In the first flurry over Lincoln's death, he was more vocal than anyone in insisting that the traitors be hung and the South punished. Later when he abruptly changed this opinion and tried to go back to an easy peace, the radicals would never forgive him.

Lincoln's funeral was held in the East Room of the White House on April 19. The black-draped casket rested on a catafalque in the center of the room. Chairs for the family had been placed at the foot but Mrs. Lincoln was indisposed and only Robert Lincoln attended. President Johnson, his Cabinet and other dignitaries were seated around the edges of the room, while Grant, in full uniform, stood alone at the head of the casket. Grant made no effort to display his usual indestructable calm. Though he maintained his rigid military bearing, he let the tears run unabashedly down his cheeks.

Personal grief would not detract from the massive work that lay ahead. Though Lee had surrendered, arrangements had to be made for other smaller units of the Confederate army to give up their arms. The afternoon following Lincoln's funeral Grant learned that Sherman was meeting in Raleigh with General Johnston and the former Confederate Secretary of War, John Breckinridge, to arrange the surrender of Johnston's forces. Two days later when Grant received a copy of Sherman's papers, he was appalled. Sherman, the scourge of the South who had burned Atlanta and marched across Georgia leaving a wake of devastation behind him, had suddenly turned into a dove of peace. Instead of merely accepting the parole of Johnston's forces, he had included terms by which the Confederate states were to be immediately readmitted to the Union with all their former political rights, a clause that far exceeded Sherman's authority as a general.

In a hasty meeting with the President and his cabinet, Stanton and Johnson were more than just appalled but went as far as to accuse Sherman of treason. Grant managed to placate them temporarily and wrote a letter to Sherman. Then, fearful of what might happen if the hot-tempered Sherman should learn of Stanton's intemperate remarks, Grant decided to deliver the letter personally. On April 24 he reached Raleigh, explained the situation to Sherman and renegotiated new terms identical to those issued to Lee.

Back in Washington, Grant sent new orders to General Phil Sheridan to take an army of fifty thousand into Louisiana and Texas to secure the surrender of Confederate General Kirby Smith in that area. There was no need of an army of that size since Smith would soon surrender without a bullet being fired; but the appearance of the large body of troops along the border was a diplomatic maneuver. While the United States had been engaged in the Civil War, the armies of Napoleon III of France had invaded Mexico, made the Archduke Maximilian of Austria Emperor of Mexico and forced the republican army of former President Benito Juárez north to the United States border. This foreign intervention in Mexico was in flagrant violation of the Monroe Doctrine, but while the Union was engaged in the Civil War, there had been little it could do. Now the appearance of Sheridan's force along the border, where they left stockpiles of ammunition to be picked up and used by the Juáristas, was aimed at giving Napoleon second thoughts. At the same time a diplomatic mission to France exerted further pressure. Napoleon withdrew his troops and by

"Let Us Have Peace"

1867 Maximilian had been defeated and executed and Mexico was a republic again.

For the remainder of 1865 and most of 1866 Grant was busy in Washington arranging for the discharge of troops, settling accounts and handling the paper work that marked the end of any war. As a hero he was called on constantly for public appearances. Grant had never had any great interest in politics and his busy routine left little time for such activities now, but it was impossible to live in Washington and not be aware of the growing animosity between President Johnson and Congress.

For several months following his inauguration Johnson had been vehement in his denunciation of the South, then his attitude had changed and he had attempted to go back to Lincoln's proposed lenient attitude. The result was a complete break between Johnson and all factions in Congress. The hardline radicals felt he had betrayed them, the moderates distrusted his sudden change in colors. Lincoln's assassination had spread its slow poison. The elections of 1866 brought more radicals into Congress, determined on an unforgiving policy toward the South, and the conflict with the President grew. These differences were not confined solely to the attitude about the South, but extended to what was considered the final authority of the government. Johnson stubbornly insisted that the President had the final say, while the members of Congress argued that they were the voice of the people and the President was subordinate to them. Both sides courted Grant's favor.

In July 1866 Congress made Grant a full general, the first man to hold that rank since George Washington. When Johnson made public appearances, he often insisted that Grant and Admiral Farragut, the two great heroes of the war, be with him as though some of their popularity might rub off on him. The new and more radical Congress elected in 1866 lost no time in making its weight felt. On March 2, 1867 it passed the Reconstruction Act over Johnson's veto, splitting the South into five military districts, with a general commanding each until such time as the states would set up new governments acceptable to Congress.

Even more obnoxious to Johnson was the passage of the Tenure of Office Act which forbade him to remove any memmer of his Cabinet without the permission of the Senate. There was nothing Johnson could do about the radicals in Congress since they had been elected by the people, but he could do something about his Cabinet. Secretary of War Stanton, who had been seeing a Confederate plot under every bed since Lincoln's death, was a staunch supporter of the radicals. As soon as Congress adjourned in the summer of 1867, Johnson asked Stanton to resign and named Grant to replace him. Grant objected, pointing out he could hardly carry on the duties of both Commander-in-Chief and Secretary of War, but when Johnson persisted, he agreed to accept the post on a temporary basis until Congress reconvened. When Congress reassembled that winter, it ordered Stanton restored. Again Grant was forced into a political battle not of his own choosing. He favored a lenient position toward the South, but he also believed that Congress was the true voice of the people and promptly turned in his resignation.

Johnson was furious. By making Grant Secretary of War he had hoped to force a Supreme Court ruling on the Tenure of Office Act, a ruling expected to go in his favor as a result of Grant's popularity. Johnson summoned Grant to the White House where, before witnesses, he accused Grant of having gone back on his word. Since the days at Jefferson Barracks when Grant had demanded an apology from Buchanan for calling him a liar, he had never been able to stand any slur against his truthfulness. Grant wrote a bitter letter to Johnson accusing him of assailing his honor and integrity and the two became enemies.

Stubbornly determined to force a Supreme Court decision, Johnson offered the position of Secretary of State to Sherman and, when he refused, named another general, Lorenzo Thomas, to the position. Congress reacted by starting impeachment proceedings. The trial dragged on for several months, ending on May 26, 1868, with Johnson being retained as President by a single vote. But his political career was already doomed. Six days earlier, on May 20, at the Republican Convention in Chicago, U. S. Grant had been nominated for President on the first ballot. Schuyler Colfax, Speaker of the House, was selected as his running mate.

Grant did not attend the convention and wrote only a short acceptance letter which made no political commitments but expressed his determination to fulfill the duties to his best abilities if elected and concluded with the statement, "Let us have peace."

The people heartily approved. They were sick of war and they were sick of the political maneuverings that had been going on in Washington since Lincoln's death. The fact that Grant had no experience in politics was construed in his favor. It was a naïve assumption. Leading an army and leading the nation were two different things and what the country really needed was a man with considerable political experience. The Democrats selected Horatio Seymour, former governor of New York, as their candidate, with Frank Blair of Missouri as his running mate.

Grant left Rawlins in charge of affairs in Washington and retired to Galena for the campaign, making no speeches or public appearances. On the evening of the election he put on an old coat and walked over to the home of Congressman Elihu Washburne, who had installed a telegraph just to receive the returns.

It was late in the evening when Grant returned home alone, removed his coat and told Julia, "I'm afraid I am elected." The vote when the final tally was completed gave him a popular majority of 3 million out of 5.7 million votes cast.

Chapter XII

The New President

The morning of March 4, 1869, was blustery and overcast in Washington, D.C., but shortly before noon the sun broke through the clouds to light up the crowds lining the streets and the two men riding in the open black phaeton in the long procession heading toward the Capitol. It was the largest crowd ever to have attended an inauguration, but many along the line of march were disappointed when they saw that Grant had put aside his uniform for a plain, dark business suit. Riding beside him in the carriage was Rawlins, his faithful aide since the days at Cairo, who now held the rank of brigadier general. Notably absent was retiring President Andrew Johnson.

Julia, their four children, Jesse Grant and almost the entire Dent family had come to Washington for the ceremonies. Only Grant's mother, shy and hating crowds, had chosen to remain at home. At the end of the procession everyone walked a short distance to the platform which had been built outside the east front of the Capitol building. As everyone took their seats, young Nellie Grant was unable to find a chair and rushed forward impulsively to seize her father's hand and stand beside him as he received an ovation from the crowd. Someone hastily located another chair and Nellie was led off as the ceremonies began with Chief Justice Salmon P. Chase administering the oath of office.

Afterward Grant stepped forward to read his inaugural address. Julia had urged him to have the speech written for him, but Grant had insisted on composing it himself, a policy he would continue throughout his Presidency. The speech was typically short and mainly expressed Grant's determination to perform his new duties to the best of his ability. Delivered in a low-pitched voice, it is doubtful that it carried much beyond the first rows, but the crowd did not seem to mind since they could read it in the newspapers later.

The Republican papers would call the speech "lucid" and "sincere." The Democrat papers would describe it variously as "arrogant," "servile" and "empty." On the whole, the public would approve of it as the speech of a simple, ordinary man like themselves.

If the inauguration was a modest success, the inaugural ball held that evening in the newly constructed wing of the Treasury Building was a complete fiasco. The crowd was larger than expected. While the President and other dignitaries managed to avoid most of the jam by remaining in an adjoining reception room, on the main floor there was not enough room for dancing, people could not reach the refreshment tables and by the time the affair was over cloaks and hats had become so hopelessly mixed up that many of the disgruntled guests had to make their way home through the freezing weather without their wraps.

Grant was not and never would be a politician. He entered office with high hopes of serving the nation well and an honest determination to do his best. The tragedy of his Presidency was that he would leave office with his name besmirched with scandal and linked to one of the most corrupt eras of American history, not through any lessening of his own integrity but because of his lack of preparedness for handling his new role.

The New President

Grant's first revelation of weakness came the morning after the inaugural ball when he released the names of his Cabinet members. During the four troubled years of the Johnson regime, Grant had been courted alternately by the radicals and the moderates. In the end the Republican Party had made him their successful Presidential candidate but, not being a politician, Grant felt no particular debt to the party. When he had been elevated to brigadier general, he had been allowed to chose his own personal staff without intervention from anyone and he chose his Cabinet in the same manner. Not only did he fail to consult the party leaders, but several leading politicians, who had expected an appointment, were completely overlooked.

Congressman Elihu Washburne, who had promoted Grant's military career, was named Secretary of State. Fortunately Grant realized that Washburne was unfitted for the job and it was only an honorary appointment with Washburne almost immediately replaced by the able and experienced Hamilton Fish. For Attorney General he selected E. Rockwood Hoar of Massachusetts, for Secretary of the Interior, Jacob D. Cox of Ohio. Hoar, Cox and Fish were all able men, but his other appointments were less pleasing. Grant's good friend Rawlins was named Secretary of War and another friend, Adolph Borie, a successful Philadelphia businessman with no naval background, was named Secretary of Navy. John A. Creswell of Maryland was made Postmaster General. Grant made his biggest blunder when he chose A. T. Stewart, an important Eastern drygoods merchant, as Secretary of the Treasury. When it was pointed out that Stewart's government contracts made it impossible for him to hold a Cabinet position, Grant reluctantly replaced him with George S. Boutwell of Massachusetts. All in all the group did not compare too unfavorably with previous Cabinets, but by his method of selection Grant had alienated many important men in Congress and revealed his political naïveté.

Grant retained the Johnson White House staff on the logical grounds that they were already trained for their jobs, but for his immediate personal staff he relied on men whom he had known from his military days. His brother-in-law, Brigadier General Fred Dent, and two former military aides, Horace Porter and Orville Babcock, presided over his outer offices at the White House, screening all applicants to see the President.

Grant had assumed office in one of the most trying times of United States history. The reconstruction of the South was going poorly, even though the Thirteenth Amendment had supposedly abolished slavery. When Congress passed the Reconstruction Act in 1867, placing the South back under military control, a flood of carpetbaggers rushed South to fill the political offices no longer available to the Southern leaders and in many cases wrest as much money as they could from the already impoverished country, which only added to the unrest.

In a further attempt to help the Negroes, ratification of the Fourteenth and Fifteenth Amendments, guaranteeing due process of law and the right to vote, had been made a requirement of the Southern states for readmission to the Union. By the time Grant took office, a number of the states had already ratified the amendments and during his administration the remaining states were readmitted and the nation was reunited again, but the problems of the carpetbaggers and abuses against the Negroes continued.

If Grant had been more experienced in political matters, he might have forced compromises on Congress, but his military background proved more of a handicap than an asset. As a military man he was accustomed to obeying orders and he believed that Congress was the voice of the people and the final authority. He presented proposals to help the Negroes and fought to institute a civil service system to help curb corruption

The New President

in government office, but when Congress failed to act, he accepted this as the will of the people.

Grant was equally inexperienced in matters concerning the stock market and high finance. As the son of an aggressive, self-made man, Grant had been brought up to admire men who were successful and all his life he had a kind of secret awe of those who were very wealthy.

The war years had been ones of enormous speculation in the United States. Fortunes had been made in government contracts and in the expansion of railroads, some acquired by honest means and others through greed and corruption. Two New York financiers, Jay Gould and Jim Fisk, had amassed personal fortunes through control of the Erie Railroad. Through a retired stockbroker, A. Rathbone Corbin, who was married to Grant's sister, Gould and Fisk were introduced to the President, and shortly after Grant took office, they came up with a new scheme to corner the gold market.

During the war the United States had gone off the gold standard so that gold was sold like wool, wheat or any other commodity on the open market. Buyers could purchase contracts for gold before it was actually produced, and if the price would be pushed up, they could turn a great profit. However, each month the Secretary of the Treasury released several million dollars in government gold on the market to pay off government bonds, which tended to keep the price steady.

Gould entertained Grant and Julia at the theater in New York and in the summer of 1869, when the President and his party traveled to the Peace Jubilee at Boston, Gould offered them the use of one of his steamboats. En route he talked to Grant about the large wheat crop which was anticipated by the farmers that fall and pointed out that, if the government would temporarily hold up on releasing gold, the rising gold price might help the farmers also. Grant admitted that he was in favor of helping the farmers, but aside from this he remained noncommittal.

Later that summer the Grants visited Saratoga Springs, the famous spa, but the visit was cut short when Grant learned that Rawlins was dying of tuberculosis. He rushed back to Washington where he remained for the rest of the summer, saddened by the loss of the man who had been his supporter and close friend for eight years. Between Rawlins' death and constantly being on public exhibition, it was a trying summer and in mid-September Grant and Julia slipped away for a few days of rest at the home of a cousin in Pennsylvania. While there Grant received a letter from Corbin asking if the government was going to keep gold off the market. Grant had Julia write a rather curt note to his sister advising her that her husband should disengage himself from any connection with Gould and Fisk. Unfortunately it was too late. Believing that they were to have a free hand, Gould and Fisk had started buying up gold in an effort to corner the market. Warned by Corbin that the government had not changed its policy, Gould withdrew, but Fisk kept on buying. By September 24 he had pushed the price of gold from 140 to 162 and was aiming at forcing it to 200. With Fisk buying up every contract in sight, other speculators rushed to join the action. When Grant received word of what was happening, he ordered the Secretary of the Treasury to release immediately $4 million in government gold. The corner on the market was thwarted and in a half hour the price of gold dropped back to 135; but hundreds of speculators had been ruined in one of the worst days of disaster on the stock market, known as Black Friday.

The crisis had been averted and a later investigation cleared Grant of any complicity, but for years his name would be linked with the scandal.

The Black Friday scandal was only the beginning. Soon Grant was to suffer another disappointment, this time in foreign policy. During his lifetime Grant had witnessed an enormous expansion of the nation's frontiers. With the land acquired from Mexico after the Mexican War and the settlement of the Oregon Territory boundary with Great Britain, the United States border had been pushed west to the Pacific Coast. During Johnson's administration Secretary of State Seward had purchased Alaska from Russia and had been considering further expansion into the Caribbean. The two small republics of Haiti and Santo Domingo (the Dominican Republic) occupied the large Caribbean island which had been known as Hispaniola in colonial days. The government of Haiti had achieved a modicum of stability, but Santo Domingo had been torn with fighting between warring factions. In 1868, when Buenaventura Baez had come into control in Santo Domingo, he had approached friends in Washington with a proposal that the country be annexed to the United States. Seward had looked with some favor on the suggestion and once Grant assumed office he took up the idea with enthusiasm. The navy was interested in acquiring Samaná Bay on the island for a coaling station, but Grant saw other possibilities. The soil of the island, devoted largely to the raising of sugar cane and tobacco, was extremely fertile. If used productively, Grant believed it could support several million colonists, possibly former slaves from the South who would be given a chance to own property and set up new states where their rights as free men would be assured. It was a well-meaning and not illogical plan, but Grant went about achieving it in entirely the wrong way.

Instead of consulting with Secretary of State Fish or Charles Sumner, chairman of the Senate Committee on Foreign Relations, Grant sent his personal aide, Orville Babcock, to deal with Baez. When Babcock returned with what amounted to a treaty for annexation of the island republic, even Grant's own Cabinet members were astounded at the unorthodox move. When the treaty was submitted to the Senate, it ran into immediate opposition. Sumner not only disapproved of Grant's methods, but he distrusted Baez's honesty and feared adverse world opinion. A commission was appointed to investigate the situation, but their efforts were minimal and Santo Domingo became a forgotten cause.

Not all of Grant's efforts met with rebuff. In one other area of foreign relations he was highly successful. During the Civil War, most of the European nations had secretly favored the South, though supposedly maintaining strict neutrality. However, when the warships *Alabama, Florida* and *Shenandoah* were built in England, then allowed to "escape" to the Azores where they were taken over by the Confederates, President Lincoln protested this flagrant violation of neutrality. While the war was in progress, little could be done, but once the war was over the United States demanded reparations from England for the damage inflicted by the warships. During Johnson's administration an agreement was reached, but when it was presented to the Senate, it was so favorable to England that it brought immediate rejection. In a violent and intemperate speech, Charles Sumner went so far as to hint that if England did not immediately settle the claims in cash, the United States should consider territorial compensation. The reaction to Sumner's speech in England was a wave of war panic with many people believing the United States intended to invade Canada.

Under Grant, negotiations with England were reopened and an American and British commission drafted the Treaty of Washington, whereby all disputes between the two nations that threatened to bring them to the brink of war were to be submitted to impartial arbitration. The Treaty of Washington was ratified by the Senate on May 24, 1869. In the case of the "Alabama claims" the King of Italy, Emperor of Brazil and President of Switzerland were selected as arbitrators. On September 14, 1869, their representatives met at Geneva, Switzer-

The New President

land, and decided in favor of the United States. They ordered England to pay $15 million in reparations. A month later, on October 21, another dispute of twenty-three years standing between the United States and Great Britain was also settled by arbitration. Though the two countries had agreed in 1846 to the extension of the boundary between the United States and Canada westward along the 49th parallel, they had continued to quarrel over the ownership of a small archipelago of islands in Puget Sound which lay directly across the parallel. With the Kaiser of Germany acting as arbitrator, these San Juan Islands were awarded to the United States.

This method of settling disputes by impartial arbitration was something entirely new in international policy and was widely acclaimed throughout Europe. Relations with Great Britain, which had been strained when Grant took office, had reached a new high of friendliness by the end of his first term.

Even in his domestic policy, Grant's first term was not without a number of progressive achievements. The first Civil Service Commission was established, though Congress refused to pass the necessary funds to make it effective; an eight-hour working day was put into effect for all government employees; and the nation's first National Park was created at Yellowstone. But before his first term was over, Grant was to be involved in still another scandal.

During Lincoln's Presidency contracts had been let for the construction of the first transcontinental railroad, with the Central Pacific building from the west and the Union Pacific from the east. On May 10, 1869, two months after Grant assumed office, the two lines were joined at Promontory Point, Utah, and the transcontinental railway became a reality. But just as Gould and Fisk had manipulated the Erie Railroad to their profit, similar manipulation had been going on within the Union Pacific. A few powerful and influential stockholders of the Union Pacific had formed their own construction company, the Credit Mobilier, and by awarding building contracts to their own company at exorbitant costs, they had diverted huge sums of government money into their own pockets. Hoping to avert any investigation by Congress, one of the stockholders had distributed shares of stock among legislators and other government officials, telling them they could pay for them later out of their profits. Sensing something wrong, some of the Congressmen had returned the stock, but others had not. When the scandal finally came into the open, many supposedly honest officials, including Vice President Colfax, were caught holding Credit Mobilier stock, and once again Grant's name was linked by association to corruption.

Though Grant was at odds with many of his own party in Congress and his name had been tainted by scandal he was still the hero of the people. In June 1872 at the Republican Convention in Philadelphia, he was nominated as the Republican candidate for a second time by acclamation. It was not the same Republican Party that he had represented four years earlier. Some of the Reform Republicans had already broken away and selected a candidate of their own, Horace Greeley, the great newspaper editor. Greeley was also chosen as the Democratic candidate. In spite of the coalition, the Reform Republicans and the Democrats had made a poor choice. Though Greeley's name was a household word because of his pithy sayings and editorials, he was also considered to be something of an eccentric and had formerly supported some unpopular causes, such as socialism, temperance and women's rights. Grant and his running mate, Henry Wilson, won the election easily with a popular majority greater than he had received before.

Chapter XIII

Second Term

March 4, 1874, dawned bitter cold with snow flurries whipped by gale-force winds and no sign of the sun breaking through a sullen sky that grew steadily darker as the line of black carriages moved down Pennsylvania Avenue toward the Capitol. If the crowd was not quite as large as that which had crammed into Washington four years earlier, it could be blamed on the freezing weather. The thousands who lined the streets, bundled in overcoats and mufflers and stamping their feet to keep warm, were testimony that Grant was still a hero to the public.

By now the Grant and Dent families had been saddened by the deaths of both Jesse Grant and Colonel Dent, but most of the other relatives and all of Grant's children were there, only Hannah Grant remaining as always in the seclusion of her home. The wind blew with such force that it ripped banners to shreds, muted the instruments of the band, causing them to give out strange, discordant notes, and almost tore Grant's inaugural address from his hands. Again he had written his own speech and his voice barely carried above the wind. "I have been the subject of abuse and slander scarcely ever equaled in political history," he told his audience, but continued with the optimistic observation that he considered his reelection proof of his vindication.

That night the inaugural ball was again packed with guests. This time there was enough room, but it was so cold that most of the guests danced in their wraps and the usual champagne and punch were overlooked in favor of coffee and hot chocolate. Even the Grants appeared relieved when a decent interval of frozen formalities had passed and everyone could escape back to the warmth of their homes.

In all the moving about during the war years, the Grants had never been able to maintain a permanent home in one place for very long. The eight years that they spent in the White House was the longest time they ever lived in the same house and they made it very much their home. By the time Grant was elected President for the first time, Fred was already a cadet at West Point. Later, Ulysses left to attend Harvard. But they returned home on leaves and vacations, and Grant and Julia visited them even more frequently. Meanwhile the younger children, Nellie and Jesse, grew up in the White House, romping through the halls, playing on the lawns and entertaining friends in the huge basement.

Grant's love of family life extended beyond Julia and the children. The White House was constantly filled with visiting Dents and Grants: brothers, sisters, cousins and their families. During Grant's first term, old Colonel Dent became almost a permanent fixture at the White House, living there for most of the year. A prominent figure at every social gathering, he sometimes embarrassed Grant's Republican friends by telling everyone that his famous son-in-law was really a Democrat at heart but just didn't know it. Jesse Grant, bursting with pride at his son's importance was also a frequent visitor, though he and Colonel Dent quarreled violently over political views. The presence of so many relatives at the White House brought charges of nepotism from Grant's enemies, but he ignored them in his pleasure at having his large family around him.

In addition to relatives, the White House was constantly filled with visitors. Those who came seeking jobs and appointments were carefully screened by Fred Dent, Horace Porter or Orville Babcock. There were so many seeking jobs that Porter once remarked wryly that if twenty men came seeking one job opening, the result was that Grant made "nineteen enemies and one ingrate." Other visitors, many of them former soldiers, came simply to talk and they were always admitted to Grant's office.

The Grants entertained a great deal. Once shy Julia developed into one of the most delightful hostesses in Washington. During the eight years in Washington, the Grants entertained many distinguished visitors, including the Prince of Wales, the Grand Duke Alexis of Russia, the Emperor of Brazil and King Kalakana of the Sandwich Islands. However, Grant always disliked formal state dinners and preferred informal dinners with friends. Shortly after the start of his second term, former Confederate General George Pickett and his wife were dinner guests. Grant and Pickett were reported to have spent the entire evening seated at the table refighting the battle of Gettysburg, writing on the tablecloth with blue pencils and using spoons to represent different divisions.

In addition to entertaining at the White House, the Grants went out a great deal to restaurants, the theater and the homes of friends, sometimes together and sometimes with Grant falling back into his old army habits of going stag in the company of other men friends.

Over the years their life developed a daily routine. Grant arose at seven and read the Washington papers. When breakfast was almost ready, he went personally to call Julia, waited for her to dress and they ate together. Afterward Grant escorted Julia to her sitting room, then took a brief stroll around the grounds smoking his cigar. By ten o'clock he was at work in his office. He maintained his office with the same air of informality that he had shown in the army. He particularly disliked the red tape of sending formal letters. If he wanted to consult with a Congressman or Senator, he snatched up his coat and strolled over to the Capitol to speak to them in person. He enjoyed chatting with ordinary people and on his walks he stopped frequently to talk to strangers.

In the afternoon when his work was done, Grant's favorite relaxation was to take a ride. Though the White House stables were full of horses—Cincinnati and Jeff Davis, Grant's favorite mounts during the war, the children's ponies, and numerous other horses—Grant seldom rode horseback anymore, but usually drove in his own carriage, at such a breakneck speed that Julia refused to accompany him.

Nellie Grant, the shy young girl who had insisted on holding her father's hand during the first inauguration, had developed into a poised, somewhat headstrong young belle of the younger social set by the time of Grant's reelection. There was criticism that she was spoiled and too much of a social butterfly. Prior to his reelection, Grant sent her on a tour of Europe. Nellie enjoyed the trip, especially the visit to England where she was presented to Queen Victoria, but on the return voyage she met and fell in love with a young Englishman, Algernon Sartoris. Grant did not entirely approve of the match, but he could not deny his daughter anything. Just two months after his second inauguration, Nellie's White House wedding was the social event of the season. The entire diplomatic corps and most of the legislators and their wives were present. There were eight bridesmaids, carefully selected from among the daughters of other prominent officials, and the Marine Band played the background music. Following the ceremonies, it was noticed that the President had disappeared. Grant was finally located sitting up in Nellie's room quietly weeping.

Second Term

During Grant's first term the family purchased a summer home on the beach at Long Branch, New Jersey—a rambling, two and a half storied house whose architecture was described as a mixture of Swiss chalet and English manor house. The Long Branch house was filled with the usual throngs of relatives and visitors, but it had an outside staircase up which children in sandy bathing clothes could reach their rooms without disturbing the President downstairs. Ships passing down the coast frequently swung in toward shore to fire a salute. The Grants usually responded by running up a flag, but when young Ulysses was home, he liked to return the salute by firing a small cannon out in front.

Though Grant usually brought sheaves of paperwork with him, he drew criticism for the hours he spent away from Washington at his summer White House. He journeyed to Long Branch mainly for Julia's sake. She hated the humid Washington summers and Long Branch was a welcome relief from the winter's social obligations. In the evenings the two often sat on the veranda with Grant holding Julia's hand in his.

In Washington Julia was constantly on display as the perfect hostess. At Long Branch she could be more informal. One evening the teen-age Ulysses abruptly broke off the conversation, jumped the rail of the porch and strolled away down the beach. His eyes twinkling, Grant turned to Julia, who was now rather plump. "Mama, if this house should catch fire and you couldn't reach the front steps, one of us would have to carry you out," he teased.

Julia made a small sniffing sound of disgust, rose, pulled up her voluminous petticoats and vaulted the porch rail as neatly as her son, while Grant roared with laughter.

If affairs of state sometimes went badly and scandal rocked around them, in their home life the Grants were able to find much happiness during the eight years in the White House. It was a happiness that meant much to Grant as the problems of his second term began. In September 1869, six months after he had begun in his first term, the nation had gone through the Black Friday scandal. In September 1873, just six months after the start of his second term, the stock market faced an even greater crisis.

Since the end of the war, the country had been riding high on a postwar boom of railroad construction, business expansion and stock speculation. Fortunes were being made on the stock market and with each new success the plungers were encouraged to expand and issue more stocks and bonds against projects that often had not even begun. Like a giant balloon the economy was blowing up larger and larger with a prosperity based more on paper than cash.

On September 17, Grant accompanied Jesse to Pennsylvania to enroll him in a private boarding school and stopped for the night at the home of Jay Cooke, one of the country's wealthiest and most influential bankers. During the evening Grant noticed that his host was called away to accept several messages, returning each time with his face more preoccupied and thoughful. But it was not until the next day, when Grant was back in Washington, that he learned the truth. Overexpanded in railroad stocks and other promotions, Cooke's bank had failed. Within days other banks, railroads and businesses were failing also, with thousands of employees thrown out of work.

Grant hurried to New York with his Secretary of the Treasury where they met with bankers, stockbrokers and financiers. All agreed that the government should act, but there were no government controls on speculation in those days and everyone had a different idea of what should be done.

The United States had suffered minor depressions previously, but that was before the great wave of industrial expansion. The panic of 1873 was more serious than any the nation had ever faced. By the end of the year more than five thousand businesses had failed. With the people demanding that the govern-

Second Term

ment do something, Congress voted to release the government's supply of greenbacks. This was the paper money that had been issued during the war and painstakingly replaced with government gold during Grant's first administration. Deep in his heart, Grant felt the issuance of this paper money was wrong. It might ease the depression temporarily, but it would cause inflation and devalue the American dollar aboard. Grant was warned that, if he vetoed the bill, it would ruin the Republican Party in the next election. Believing Congress was the true voice of the people, Grant briefly persuaded himself that it was his duty to sign the bill and he composed the speech that he planned to deliver when he signed it. When he reread the speech, he laid it aside. It was the first time Grant had knowingly gone against what he believed to be the will of the people, but with only one day left to act, he tore up his speech and sent the bill back with his veto.

The veto lost him thousands of supporters. It also lost the Republicans the midterm elections, so that for the remaining two years of his administration Grant had to battle an antagonistic Democratic Congress. Gradually the stock market leveled off, a small quantity of greenbacks was released, and the nation slowly began to work its way back to normalcy.

Added to the hostility of Congress, Grant's last two years in office were marked by new scandals. General William W. Belknap had succeeded Rawlins as Grant's Secretary of War. On March 2, 1876, Belknap appeared at Grant's office and tendered his resignation. The following day the story broke in all the papers. Belknap in his position as Secretary of War had the job of appointing Indian agents, and since he had taken office, his first wife and later her sister had been receiving kickbacks from one of the Indian agencies. At the ensuing trial, Belknap insisted that he had not known of his wife's behind-the-scene dealings and was acquitted, but not before a new scandal had swept Washington.

Even more painful to Grant was the uncovering of the infamous Whiskey Ring. To help pay off the war debt, high taxes had been levied on whiskey and all distilled spirits. An investigation by the Secretary of the Treasury uncovered the fact that a network of government officials, from minor officers in the revenue service up to others in high position, had been falsifying reports on the amounts of whiskey produced in return for bribes from the whiskey distillers. Warned that the investigation might lead to those close to him, Grant still sent orders: "Let no guilty man escape." But he was not prepared for the disclosures that his own personal aide, Orville Babcock, was among the accused. Loyal to his friend, Grant appeared as a character witness at Babcock's trial and he, too, was acquitted, but the scandal remained.

When Grant had taken office, his sentiments had been allied with the moderate Republicans, who favored a lenient attitude toward the South, but he was also a champion of Negro rights. As the years passed with continued antagonism with the South over enforcement of the Fifteenth Amendment, giving the Negroes the right to vote, people became weary of the constant fighting and there was a changing attitude toward forgetting the whole issue and letting the South settle its own problems. Only the Republican radicals in Congress kept the issue alive with violent speeches denouncing the treatment being given the Negroes, a policy which was given the derisive name of "waving the bloody shirt." By the close of his second term of office, Grant's principal supporters had become these hard-line, radical Republicans.

In 1876 they urged Grant to run for still a third term. Julia was in favor of it, but Grant did not agree. Beneath his surface calm, the scandals and barbs had hurt him deeply. The newspapers were raking up the old scandals and even hinting that he planned to set himself up as monarch. "Down with Caesar-

Second Term

ism. No King. No Emperor. No Third Term!" they screamed in their editorials. Grant informed the Republicans he would not run.

There were many willing to take his place. So many that the Republicans meeting in June 1876 at Cincinnati had to compromise on a dark-horse candidate, Rutherford B. Hayes, a former general in the army and three times governor of Ohio. Two weeks later at their convention in St. Louis the Democrats nominated Samuel J. Tilden of New York.

As the returns began coming in on election night, it appeared that Tilden was getting the majority of the popular vote, but it required 185 electoral votes to win and Tilden could only produce 184. Immediately preceding the election, a wave of anti-Negro feeling had swept the South with stepped-up activities by the Ku Klux Klan aimed at keeping the Negroes from the polls. As a result, the ballots from South Carolina, Florida and Louisiana were disputed. These, along with the vote from Oregon which had not yet come in, would be enough to give Hayes the electoral majority.

As weeks passed and no decision was made, a new wave of unrest swept the country. There were riots in the South, and in New York there was talk of inaugurating Tilden even if it meant seceding from the Union. As a military man Grant acted to curb the unrest by threatening to put New York under siege if necessary and sending Sherman orders to put down any rebellion in the South. The crisis passed and the decision was placed in the hands of Congress. On March 2, 1877, Hayes was announced the winner. Prior to this, numerous statesmen had visited the South and in time it became obvious that a "deal" had been made. With promises to remove the army from the South and no longer be so strenuous in demanding enforcement of the Fifteenth Amendment, the Southern Democrats had been pacified.

So with another scandal that would not be uncovered until years later by historians, Grant left office, weary of the whole business and a little bewildered that so many good intentions had gone so completely astray. A master at the game of war, he had proved a novice in the game of politics.

Chapter XIV

Ambassador to the World

Tugboats, steamships and private yachts filled the air with a cacophony of blasting whistles as the transatlantic steamer *Indiana* swung away from her Philadelphia berth and started down the Delaware River toward Delaware Bay and the Atlantic Ocean. The cheers of the thousands of people gathered on the wharf drowned out the music of the band.

If Grant had left the White House under a cloud of scandal, one never would have guessed it now. On May 17, 1877, it seemed as though all of Philadelphia had gathered to see the ex-president off on a tour of Europe. Long after Julia and Jesse had retired to their stateroom, Grant remained on deck waving his hat in salute to the flotilla of small craft that escorted the steamship down the river.

In early March at a quiet, informal dinner the Grants had turned over the keys to the White House to Rutherford B. Hayes, and once again Grant had faced the future, much as he had in 1854 on leaving Fort Humboldt, a man without a job or definite plans. There was an important difference now, however. He was a world-famed figure, and though far from a millionaire, he was substantially wealthy. Grant had always loved to travel. During his eight years as President he had sent

Nellie, Fred and Ulysses on trips abroad and entertained important guests from all over the world. Now he intended to see something of that world himself. In England they would visit Nellie and her husband. Behind them they were leaving Fred, now a colonel on General Sherman's staff, and Ulysses, a young businessman in New York. Before departing Grant had entrusted Ulysses with $100,000, which represented most of the family funds, with plans to return when this money began to run out.

Grant was fifty-five and the years had altered his appearance. No longer lean and wiry, he had added some twenty pounds in weight. There was a heavy sprinkling of gray in his hair and beard and he now required glasses for reading. He was better dressed, usually appearing in a dark frock coat with a heavy gold watch chain across his vest and wearing a tall silk hat, but his face was still a leathery tan from the long years in the open and his pockets bulged with the customary cigars. Once the formalities of the departure were over, Grant appeared to be everywhere on shipboard, talking to the other passengers, examining the vessel from bow to stern and showing all the exuberance of a schoolboy on a holiday.

On May 27 they reached Cóbh, Ireland, and the following day put into Liverpool. At both places the ships in the harbors were decorated with flags and bunting and thousands of people lined the piers to greet them. The scandals that had surrounded Grant's Presidency back home meant little in Europe. To the people of Europe he was still the great hero because of his record in the Civil War.

Alerted by the crowds which had gathered at Philadelphia to see Grant off, the New York *Herald,* previously one of Grant's severest critics, had arranged to put a reporter, John Russell Young, aboard the *Indiana* at Cóbh. Young would remain with Grant throughout the tour, sending back daily accounts to the newspapers, which eventually would be published in two massive volumes, *Around the World with General Grant*.

Wherever the Grants stopped in England, the enthusiastic reception was the same, with children waving banners reading "Welcome, General Grant" or "Let Us Have Peace" and bands playing "The Star Spangled Banner" and "John Brown's Body," which was considered Grant's special theme song. Though Grant had never enjoyed public speaking, he amazed everyone with a new talent for extemporaneous speech making. While in England the Grants were entertained by the Prince of Wales and Queen Victoria. In spite of all the pomp and solemnity that marked most of these public appearances, Grant did not lose his sense of humor. On June 15 he was presented the keys to London and honored at a banquet at the Crystal Palace, followed by a display of fireworks. One of the pyrotechnic displays was a portrait of Grant himself, followed by a blazing picture of the United States Capitol. "They have burnt me in effigy, and now they are burning the Capitol," Grant observed with a grin to those sitting next to him.

On July 4, the Grants wound up their London visit at a party given by the American legation. By now the social season was ending in London and they decided to spend the remaining summer months on the Continent.

They crossed the Channel to Ostend, Belgium, where King Leopold visited them at their hotel, then greeted them a few days later at more formal ceremonies in Brussels. While there, a message arrived from Chancellor Otto von Bismarck of Germany explaining that the aged Kaiser Wilhelm, who was recovering from an assassination attempt, was too ill to see them, but he was sending a personal representative to escort them on a tour of Germany. King Leopold's private railway car carried them to the German border where they met their new escort, who took them on a cruise down the Rhine. They visited Switzerland, crossed the Alps into northern Italy and by late August returned to England.

On this second visit to England they went to Scotland, stopping at Edinburgh, Glasgow and Granton, the home of Grant's Scottish ancestors, and spent several weeks with Nellie and her husband. Though Grant was politely appreciative of the many museums and art galleries that they visited, it was obvious that he was much more interested in the scenery of Europe and its people. In England he particularly enjoyed walking the streets and talking to the people. While addressing a crowd at Birmingham, he mentioned his personal dream that someday "the nations of the earth would agree on some sort of Congress which shall take cognizance of international questions of difficulty and whose decisions will be as binding as the decisions of our Supreme Court are binding on us."

In late October, the Grants returned to France where more receptions and honors were waiting. While Julia was having some gowns made by French dressmakers, Grant escaped to the foreign offices of the New York *Herald*, where he spent his time catching up on the back news in the American papers.

By now Young's reports of the trip were being published throughout the United States and the government realized that in Grant they had one of the most valuable goodwill ambassadors the United States had ever sent abroad. Early in December the *Vandalia* a United States warship currently cruising in the Mediterranean, was put at Grant's disposal so that he could continue the tour throughout the Mediterranean.

The Grants boarded the *Vandalia* at Nice on December 13. Cruising down the coast of Italy, they made shore trips to see Mount Vesuvius, which refused to put on a volcanic display for them, and to historic Pompeii, where a house was excavated just in honor of their coming. They spent Christmas at Palermo aboard the warship, then set sail across the Mediterranean for Egypt. On the crossing they ran into a violent storm and Julia

Ambassador to the World

ventured up on deck long enough to beg the captain to drop anchor. The embarrassed captain was trying to explain that this was impossible in midocean when Grant arrived and led his wife back to their cabin, explaining wryly that even he would not presume to give orders to a ship's captain. Grant did not seem to mind the rough passage. While the rest of the party were sick in their cabins, he spent the crossing rereading Mark Twain's *The Innocents Abroad*.

They arrived in Alexandria in time for Grant to enjoy a dinner with the famous explorer Henry M. Stanley, who was just returning from the heart of Africa: then, accompanied by the director of the Egyptian Museum, they took a cruise up the Nile to visit the Pyramids and ancient ruins. Grant exchanged his top hat for an Indian helmet while Julia donned a wide-brimmed straw hat, protecting her face with many veils and blue-tinted glasses.

Back aboard the *Vandalia* again, they continued on to Beirut, Damascus and Constantinople (Istanbul), Turkey. In Greece they were entertained by the King and Queen and the Parthenon was especially lighted for them at night. In Rome Grant was received by the Pope and King Humberto.

Throughout the journey Grant had been asked many times to participate in military reviews but had managed to excuse himself by explaining that he no longer wanted any connection with anything relating to war. But in Milan he found it impossible to get out of reviewing Italy's crack regiment, the "flying Bersaglieri," so named because the foot soldiers performed most of their intricate maneuvers on the run. Several Italian officers in full dress uniform escorted a spirited bay horse to the hotel where Grant was staying. When Grant appeared, a short, rather portly man in a black frock coat who had to be helped onto his mount, their disappointment was evident. Once in the saddle, Grant showed that he had not forgotten his horsemanship. For more than an hour he rode at a full gallop, putting the Bersaglieri through their maneuvers while the onlookers cheered continuously.

From Italy the Grants returned to France, where they left the *Vandalia*. By June they had reached Germany again, where they were entertained by both Bismarck and Crown Prince Frederick, though the Kaiser was still not permitted to see visitors. Continuing on through the Scandinavian countries of Denmark, Norway and Sweden, they stopped to visit the Czar in Russia, then swung south to Austria where Grant dined with the Emperor Franz Joseph. While in Vienna, word reached him that the Kaiser was sufficiently recovered to see him. Leaving the rest of the party, Grant returned by rail to Germany to spend an evening with Kaiser Wilhelm.

By October the tour had reached Spain, where they remained for two months, making numerous side trips to visit Portugal, the British fortress of Gibraltar and the tomb of Ferdinand and Isabella in Granada. Julia was particularly impressed with the little jewel box from which Queen Isabella had supposedly taken the jewels that paid for Columbus' voyage. She was less impressed with Isabella's crown, which was unadorned with jewels, heavy and made of solid silver so blackened with age that it looked like iron. The guide insisted on placing the crown on Julia's head, but when Reporter Young teased her by saying, "I'm going to wire the *Herald* tonight that Julia Grant is in Europe trying on crowns," she took it off hastily. The Grants still remembered those headlines in the newspapers: "No King . . . No Third Term."

By now Grant and Julia had been away from the United States for a year and a half. Twenty-year-old Jesse was growing tired of traveling and Julia was secretly homesick, but Grant was enjoying every minute. They had never intended to stay this long, but money was no longer a problem. The funds they had left with Ulysses had been nearly doubled through investments suggested by a young New York stockbroker, Ferdinand

Ward. But the real decision was made when word arrived from the United States government that the warship *Richmond* would soon be leaving Mediterranean waters to go through the Suez Canal to the Orient and it had been given orders to pick up the former President and his party if he wished to complete his tour by traveling around the world and returning home by way of San Francisco.

Julia put aside her own homesickness in deference to Grant's enthusiasm. They hurried back to England where Jesse was sent home to reenter school. While Julia visited with Nellie again, Grant rushed off for a belated trip to Ireland. When Grant rejoined Julia in Paris early in January, 1879, he found to his surprise that his eldest son, Colonel Fred Dent, and former Secretary of the Navy Adolph Borie had arrived to accompany them for the remainder of the tour.

Since the *Richmond* had not yet made its appearance, they traveled by private steamer across the Mediterranean and boarded a smaller steamer which would take them down the Red Sea and through the Suez Canal into the Indian Ocean. For the first time they were traveling as private citizens without all the fanfare that had greeted them as state visitors and Grant was hoping it might continue. But word of their arrival had raced ahead of them. As they steamed into the harbor at Bombay, once again they saw every ship decorated with flags and a huge crowd of Indian and British officials were waiting to whisk them off to Government House on Malabar Point to be the guests of the British government.

At Malabar Point the guests were given individual cottages set among lush gardens shaded by mango trees. Native servants were everywhere. Whenever a guest ventured out of his cottage, a servant would spring forward with an umbrella to shield him from the hot Indian sun. Some of the party jokingly gave their cottages nicknames. That occupied by Borie was called Tiger Hall and Young's cottage was Cobra Castle. Julia had heard about India's cobras. Shortly after her arrival she was heard screaming from her bath. To her embarrassment, but the relief of the native servants, the cobra which she thought she had seen coiled in a corner was only one of her own carelessly discarded silk stockings.

From Bombay the Grants boarded a railway train to travel across India. Along the way they were entertained by maharajas, local princes and English officials. They saw the Taj Mahal at Agra, stopped at the holy city of Benares, rode on elephant back and in camel carts and visited Lucknow, where a hundred elephants in rich trapping were lined up along the road to salute them with raised trunks. By early March they had reached Calcutta, where they were the guests of Lord Lytton, the Viceroy of India.

Learning that the *Richmond* had not yet passed through the Suez Canal, Grant insisted on making new stops in Siam (Thailand), Burma, French Indochina (Vietnam) and Singapore. Continuing up the coast of China, they reached Shanghai on May 17. While the guns of the Woosung forts greeted them with a twenty-one-gun salute, the American man-of-war *Monocacy* steamed out to escort them into the harbor. After four days at Shanghai they sailed up the Yellow Sea to Tientsin to meet Viceroy Li-Hung-chang, head of the Chinese armies and the most influential man in China next to the royal family. Li and Grant took an immediate liking to each other. At about the same time that the Civil War was being fought in the United States, Li had led the forces that put down the Taiping Rebellion in China and the Viceroy likened the two conflicts to each other in that both had threatened to tear their respective countries asunder.

Li also made arrangements for the Grants to visit the walled capital of Peking, a courtesy rarely granted foreign visitors. The trip was made upriver aboard a flotilla of small flatboats, then Grant was transferred to horseback and Julia to a covered palanquin for another hard day's journey overland. From the high walls surrounding Peking they were able to look across to the yellow walls and tiled roofs of the Imperial Palace, which was considered sacred ground and forbidden to everyone except those in attendance on the Emperor. Since the Emperor of China was then a boy only seven years of age, he was not considered old enough to receive state visitors, but the Grants were entertained by Prince Kung, the Regent. In the course of their talks, the Prince expressed his concern over the string of Loochoo (Ryuku) Islands which had been considered a part of China but had recently been taken over by the Japanese. Grant explained that as a private citizen he had no power to mediate but promised that he would mention the matter to the Emperor of Japan.

By now the *Richmond* had caught up with them and, boarding the warship, they sailed for Nagasaki, Japan, where they were greeted with another twenty-one-gun salute. During the week that they remained in Nagasaki, the city's sky blazed every night with fireworks in their honor, and they were entertained at a fifty-course dinner given by the local merchants and took part in a tree-planting ceremony commemorating Japanese-American friendship.

Leaving Nagasaki, the *Richmond* steamed up the Sea of Japan to Yokohama, where Emperor Mutsuhito's private railway car was waiting to carry them to the summer palace at Tokyo. The emperor had chosen the following day, which was the Fourth of July, to receive them officially. The reception was extremely formal with the young emperor dressed in full uniform and the empress in ruby velvet. Mutsuhito bowed formally to the other members of the party, but broke all precedent by coming forward to shake Grant's hand. A few days later he broke precedent again by having Grant sit beside him at a review of Japanese troops. Because of a cholera epidemic then sweeping Japan, the Grants were not allowed to visit the interior, but they remained in Japan for two months. During several private talks with the emperor, Grant found occasion to mention the problem of the Loochoo Islands and the emperor assured him that he would take whatever steps he could without lowering Japanese dignity to allay China's fears. Of all their many stops around the world, Grant considered the stay in Japan the most satisfying because of the new bonds of friendship that were established with the United States.

But all trips must eventually come to an end. By now even Grant was beginning to show signs of homesickness. On August 29 he presented his farewell remarks to the emperor and on September 3, 1879, the Grants boarded the American steamship *City of Tokyo* and set sail for San Francisco and home. The trip had extended for more than two years and had included meetings with the leaders of most of the major countries of the world.

Chapter XV

The Last Battle

During the twenty-eight months Grant had been abroad, John Young's serialized accounts of his travels had been read with great interest at home. On September 20, 1879, when the *City of Tokyo* put into San Francisco, there was another tumultuous welcome with salutes from the naval vessels in the bay and crowds thronging the docks. Grant and Julia visited Yosemite in California, stopped at Virginia City and Carson City, Nevada, and continued east with more celebration at Cheyenne, Omaha, Galena and finally Chicago, where the veterans of the Army of the Tennessee had gathered for a reunion and General Sheridan led a parade past Grant on the reviewing stand.

Grant's travels still were not over. After resting briefly early in 1880, he and Julia took off again visiting several cities in the South, Cuba and finally Mexico, where they were the personal guests of Mexico's President, General Porfirio Diáz. It was late spring before they finally returned to Galena.

By now another Presidential election was rapidly approaching. The administration of Rutherford Hayes had not been a particularly successful one and a number of the old-line Republicans had seized on Grant's continuing popularity and were suggesting him for President again.

At first Grant was reluctant. "They have designs on me which I do not contemplate myself," he observed, but Julia was in favor of the idea and gradually her enthusiasm and that of their friends spread to Grant also. He felt that the many contacts he had made on his trip around the world had given him valuable new insights for handling the important office.

When the Republican convention opened in Chicago on June 2, Grant did not attend, but he let it be known that he would accept the nomination. Roscoe Conkling, Senator from New York, put his name in nomination while Senator James A. Garfield of Ohio nominated his fellow Ohio Senator, John Sherman. On the first ballot Grant received 304 votes, with 378 necessary for the nomination. On successive ballots Grant's count crept up slightly but not enough to win the nomination. When it began to appear that the convention was deadlocked, some of Sherman's and Grant's supporters met in a closed meeting and a wire was sent to Grant suggesting that, if he promised to make Sherman Secretary of the Treasury, he might be persuaded to throw his votes to Grant. Infuriated at this evidence of behind-the-scene dealings, Grant wired back: "It was my intention, if nominated and elected, to appoint John Sherman Secretary of the Treasury. Now you may be certain I shall not. Not to be President of the United States would I consent that such a bargain should be made."

Grant had predicted his own defeat. He was not to be President again. On the thirty-sixth ballot, the convention broke the deadlock by nominating Garfield, a dark-horse candidate on whom all could agree. Garfield went on to win the Presidency over Winfield Hancock Scott, the Democratic nominee. Within six months after his nomination, Garfield had been assassinated by a disgruntled office seeker and Vice President Chester A. Arthur became President.

The failure to receive the nomination was a disappointment to the entire Grant family. Julia was openly heartbroken, but

The Last Battle

Grant kept his inner feelings to himself and supported Garfield in his campaign. In December Grant and Julia were guests at a dinner given by President Hayes, and following Garfield's assassination, they were guests of honor at the first state dinner given by President Arthur. But Grant's political career was over and there was no real place for him in Washington. Over the years the Grants had purchased White Haven from Colonel Dent and houses in Galena, Long Branch and Philadelphia, but by now most of their friends seemed to be living in the East. Moving to New York City, they purchased a house on East 66th Street just off fashionable Fifth Avenue. A four-storied brownstone with large bay windows facing the street, it was filled as always with their visiting children, grandchildren and the usual throngs of relatives. During the tour abroad, the money young Ulysses had invested on the advice of Ferdinand Ward had done very well, so Grant joined with Ward in forming the Grant and Ward banking house. Ward was the director of the firm with Ulysses, Jr., an active partner. Grant and James F. Fish, Ward's father-in-law and president of the Marine Bank of Brooklyn, were silent partners. Grant's name was enough to encourage people to invest in the firm.

The next four years were happy years for Grant. There was ample time for visiting with old friends and his family. Every summer they journeyed to Long Branch, where Nellie joined them from England with her three children. Whenever Grant grew bored of entertaining family and friends, he could always make a show of business by going downtown to spend a few hours in the private office set aside for him at the firm of Grant and Ward. According to Ward, the firm was prospering with huge dividends from railroad investments, high rates of interest charged to contractors and a steadily growing reserve fund which was kept in the Marine Bank.

On May 4, 1884, Grant was surprised by a visit from Ward at his home. Ward explained that an unexpectedly large city draft against the Marine Bank was threatening to close that bank's doors in the morning. If the bank did not open, their reserve fund could be lost. Ward had already raised $250,000 to cover the draft, but another $150,000 was needed. Since it was a Sunday, there was only one place Grant could secure a large sum on quick notice. He borrowed the money from his long-time friend, wealthy Cornelius Vanderbilt, giving Vanderbilt his personal check which was to be cashed as soon as the bank had passed the crisis.

Monday passed with no hint of trouble. On Tuesday, May 6, Grant drove downtown to the firm office where Ulysses, Jr., white-faced and stunned looking, met him at the door. "Grant and Ward have failed and Ward has fled," he cried. Climbing the stairs to his office, Grant sat there alone for several hours with his head buried in his hands. Not only was he penniless, but the failure had wiped out the savings of the rest of his family as well as those of the hundreds of investors who had trusted his good name. By the close of the day he knew there was no mistake. There were no securities or high-interest loans, no reserve in the Marine Bank, Ward had simply cleared out and absconded with everything.

Grant's personal account was so low that only the fortuitous gifts of several thousand dollars from secret admirers enabled the family to pay their household bills those next few months. The personal debt to Vanderbilt bothered Grant the most. He retained the titles to the New York house and Long Branch, since they both were in Julia's name, but White Haven and the rest of their property in Galena, Philadelphia and Chicago he turned over to Vanderbilt, along with all his war relics. Vanderbilt tried to refuse or at least get Julia to allow him to put the property in a trust in her name, but Julia was as adamant as her husband about paying the obligation. Vanderbilt finally accepted the deeds but returned the relics, which Julia packed up a few weeks later and sent to the Smithsonian Institution.

The Last Battle

Grant still faced the problem of finding some way to support his family. By now twenty years had passed since the Civil War and there was a current revival of interest in the war, particularly for the memoirs of prominent men who had served in it. Grant had been approached earlier by the editors of *The Century* magazine to write several articles, but he had refused because he believed he had no literary talent and because one of his friends, General Adam Badeau, had already published a three-volume work, *Military History of Ulysses S. Grant,* which had not sold very well. Now *The Century* magazine approached him again, pointing out that Grant's story told in his own words might have much greater appeal. Grant agreed to give it a try and wrote two articles on Shiloh and Vicksburg. They were so well received that he agreed to write two more on Chattanooga and the Wilderness and consider writing a book.

About this time Grant had a visit from Mark Twain, who had long been one of Grant's admirers. One of the leading literary figures in the United States, Mark Twain had just formed his own publishing company along with his nephew, Charles L. Webster. He asked to be allowed to publish Grant's *Memoirs,* offering him a much higher rate than the Century Company and promising to promote advance sales by subscription, which would start bringing in money immediately. An agreement was reached with the Century Company for Charles Webster to take over the publication. Grant threw himself into the task with enthusiasm.

One room of the house was set aside as his study. At night he made notes, the next morning dictated them to a secretary, then went over them making notations, corrections and additions. Soon the first section of the book, which was to be in two volumes, was on its way to the printers.

Before Grant had progressed far into the work, he learned that he was fighting his last battle. All summer he had been troubled with a sore throat, with each doctor sending him to another without a definite diagnosis. In October he visited Dr. Hancock Douglas, who had attended Rawlins during his last illness, and Douglas told him the truth: He had cancer of the throat with no possibility of a cure.

Accepting the verdict, Grant returned home and began a battle against time to finish the two volumes and leave behind him some means of support for his family. The cancer spread rapidly. It became more and more difficult for him to eat and he began to lose weight. When his voice failed, he gave up dictating and wrote by himself on pads of paper held on his lap. In December, Fred resigned from the army and moved into the house to assist him. Later Nellie came from England to help Julia. By February, 1885 Grant had lost sixty pounds and was being attended by a staff of physicians with daily cocaine washes applied to his throat to try to ease the pain. The newspapers set up a press office in a house across the street and began issuing daily bulletins on his condition.

Confined to a special chair where he sat swathed in blankets with a small black skullcap on his head, Grant kept on writing. His visitors had to be screened, but Sherman called frequently and Sheridan and former Confederate General Simon Bolivar Buckner came to see him. Some visitors went away saying the book was killing him, others that it was all that kept him alive. When the first volume was finished, Twain was able to report that the advance sales at $3.50 a copy were already guaranteeing $250,000.

Once the newspapers began issuing daily reports on Grant's condition, people came by the hundreds to walk by the house or stand outside. Occasionally Grant went to the window and lifted his hand in salute, but his time was precious now and most of it was devoted to finishing the book. As summer approached, the doctors advised a change in climate and a friend offered his home at Mount McGregor, New York, near Sara-

The Last Battle

toga Springs. Vanderbilt sent his private railway carriage and Grant, wan and pale and swathed in robes, was helped aboard. As the train wound its way up the Hudson River, he asked to be assisted to the window, where he stood looking across the river to the gray walls of West Point until they had dropped from sight. It was too far for him to see them, but the entire cadet corps was drawn up at attention in honor of the train's passing.

The house at Mount McGregor was too small to hold all the family so some were housed at the Balmoral Hotel nearby. Seated in a chair on the veranda, Grant continued his writing. By now he had given up pen and ink and white writing paper and was writing in pencil on a yellow tablet. He no longer stopped for corrections and deletions; others would have to take care of those later. But he was winning his battle. By July 21, it had been completed.

For weeks Grant had been sleeping half-seated in a large chair with his legs supported on another. On the evening of July 22 he asked to be carried to his bed, which the doctors and family accepted as a bad sign. Throughout the night Julia and his four children kept a vigil by his bed as his pulse grew steadily weaker. Around eight on the morning of July 23, 1885, he stopped breathing, so quietly that the doctor had to wait a short interval to be certain that he was gone. Pinned inside Grant's robe they found a note he had written two weeks earlier. Addressed to Julia, it advised her to take good care of their children and concluded with the words "With these few injunctions and the knowledge I have of your love and affection and the dutiful affection of all our children, I bid you a final farewell, until we meet in another and I trust better world. You will find this on my person after my demise."

Following private family services, Grant's body was carried aboard a crepe-draped train to New York where it lay in state until the formal funeral services on August 8. Four of the pall-bearers had been selected by Grant himself: Generals Sherman and Sheridan, representing the Union, and Generals Buckner and Johnston, representing the Confederacy. The others were selected by President Grover Cleveland from among Grant's friends. Over a million people lined the streets to watch as the black-draped caisson drawn by twenty-four black horses rolled to the cemetery on Riverside Drive.

Grant's *Memoirs,* when finally published, brought even more than anticipated, enough to keep Julia and the children in comfort.

Over the ensuing years thousands of visitors came to pay their respects at Grant's original tomb, a simple, homely monument of red brick. On April 27, 1897, the day that would have been Grant's seventy-fifth birthday, the magnificent tomb where he now lies, built almost entirely by public donation including the pennies of schoolchildren, was formally dedicated by President McKinley.

Grant had chosen to be buried in the cemetery on Riverside Drive rather than at West Point so that Julia could be buried beside him. On her death in 1902, her casket was also placed in the tomb. Over the entranceway are inscribed the words "Let Us Have Peace." They remain a lasting tribute to the reluctant warrior, who hated war and did not want to be a soldier, but became the most famous general of his time.

SUGGESTED FURTHER READING

Catton, Bruce, *Grant Moves South*. Boston: Little-Brown, 1960.

────── *Grant Takes Command*. Boston: Little-Brown, 1968.

────── *U. S. Grant and the American Military Tradition*. New York: Universal Library, Grosset & Dunlap, 1954.

Grant, U. S., *Personal Memoirs of U. S. Grant,* 2 vols. New York: Charles Webster, 1885.

Grant, U. S. 3rd. *Ulysses S. Grant: Warrior and Statesman*. New York: William Morrow, 1969.

Lewis, Lloyd, *Captain Sam Grant*. Boston: Little-Brown, 1950.

Meredith, Roy, ed., *Mr. Lincoln's General, U. S. Grant: An Illustrative Autobiography*. New York: Dutton, 1959.

Meyer, Howard N., *The Life of Ulysses S. Grant*. New York: Crowell-Collier, 1967.

Randall, Ruth Painter, *Lincoln's Sons*. Boston: Little-Brown, 1955.

Ross, Isabel. *The General's Wife: The Life of Mrs. Ulysses S. Grant*. New York: Dodd-Mead, 1959.

Woodward, W. E., *Meet General Grant*. New York: Horace Liveright, 1928.

INDEX

Alabama, 108, 112
Alabama, 154
"Alabama claims," 154-155
Alaska, 153
Alleghenies, 7, 110
Ampudia, Pedro de, 50, 52
Anna, Santa, 36, 53-56, 58
Appomattox Courthouse, 135, 139
Appomattox River, 129, 134
Appomattox Station, 134, 135
Arkansas, 103
Army of the Cumberland, 113
Army of the Ohio, 94, 101, 102, 109
Army of the Potomac, 77, 94, 101, 108, 114, 118, 121, 123, 125, 126, 131
Army of the Tennessee, 92, 98, 101, 123, 177
Around the World with General Grant, 169
Arthur, Chester A., 178, 179
Atlanta, 130, 131, 132, 141
Austria, 172

Babcock, Orville, 135, 136, 150, 153, 159, 164
Baez, Buenaventura, 153-154
Bailey, Bart, 18, 19
Banks, Nathaniel P., 105, 106, 109, 110, 120, 130
Baton Rouge, 102
Beauregard, P. T., 94, 101
Belgium, 169
Belknap, William W., 163
Belle Memphis, 82, 83
Belmont, 82-84

Benton, Jessie, 37
Benton, Thomas Hart, 37
Bethel, 28, 31, 32, 36, 60, 61, 62, 67
Bismarck, Otto von, 169, 172
Black Fort, 50-52
Black Friday, 152, 162
Blair, Frank, 145
Booth, John Wilkes, 140
Borie, Adolph, 149, 173
Boutwell, George S., 149
Bowers, T. S., 136-137
Bragg, Braxton, 59, 101, 102, 109, 112, 114, 115-117, 121
Breckinridge, John, 141
Brinton, John H., 80
Brown, Jacob, 45
Brown, John, 10, 69, 134
Brown, Owen, 10
Brown County, 7
Brown's Ferry, 112-114
Brownsville, 45
Buchanan, James, 68
Buchanan, Robert, 33, 34-35, 66-67, 144
Buckner, Simon Bolivar, 28, 67, 85, 89, 91-92, 93, 104, 182, 184
Buell, Don Carlos, 25, 59, 84, 85, 86, 88, 92, 94-97, 101, 102, 109
Buena Vista, 53
Bull Run, first battle of, 75, 77, 121
Burlington, 139, 140
Burnside, Ambrose, 103-104, 110, 112, 117, 127

Cairo, Illinois, 77, 78, 79, 80, 81, 84, 86, 87, 99, 107, 110, 147

186

INDEX

California, 36, 58, 61, 62, 63, 65, 76, 177
Camp Salubrity, 38, 39
Canada, 46, 64, 154, 155
Caribbean, 153
Central Pacific, 155
Century, The, 181
Cerro Gordo, 54, 55
Chancellorsville, 108
Chapultepec, 56, 57
Chase, Salmon P., 148
Chattanooga, 101, 109, 110, 111, 112, 115, 117, 118, 181
Chickamauga Creek, 109
Chickasaw Bluffs, 103, 106
China, 174-175
Cincinnati, 9, 15, 28, 32, 67, 72, 165
City of Tokyo, 176, 177
Civil Service Commission, 155
Clay, Henry, 17, 39
Clermont County, 28
Cleveland, Grover, 184
Cóbh, Ireland, 168
Cold Harbor, 128, 129, 130
Colfax, Schuyler, 145, 156
Columbia River, 64, 65
Confederate Army of Northern Virginia, 121, 124, 135
Confederate Army of Tennessee, 120
Confederate Army of the West, 132
Conkling, Roscoe, 178
Connecticut, 9
Cooke, Joy, 162
Corbin, A. Rathbone, 151, 152
Corinth, 94, 98, 100-102, 103
Corpus Christi, 40
Covington, 67
Cox, Jacob D., 149
Credit Mobilier, 156
Creswell, John A., 149
Cuba, 177
Cumberland River, 85, 88

Dana, Charles, 111, 113
Davis, Jefferson, 67, 94, 107, 131
Dent, Ellen, 34
Dent, Emily, 34, 60
Dent, Colonel Frederick, 34, 37-38, 39, 60, 61, 67, 68, 157, 158, 179

Dent, Frederick, 29, 33, 41, 57, 150, 159
Dent, Mrs. Frederick, 34, 68
Dent, George, 34
Dent, Louis, 34
Detroit, 61
Díaz, Porifiro, 177
Dorn, Earl Van, 25, 102
Douglas, Hancock, 182

Early, Jubal, 130, 131-132
Egypt, 170-171
Emancipation Proclamation, 107
Erie Railroad, 151, 155
Ewell, Richard S., 25

Farragut, David G., 102, 131, 143
Fifteenth Amendment, 150, 164, 165
Fillmore, Millard, 68
Fish, Hamilton, 149, 153
Fish, James F., 179
Fisk, Jim, 151, 152, 155
Florida, 70, 169
Florida, 154
Floyd, John B., 89, 91
Ford Theater, 139, 140
Foote, Andrew, 81, 86, 87-91, 93
Fort Donelson, 85, 88-92, 93
Fort Heiman, 85, 86, 87
Fort Henry, 85, 86-88, 89, 93, 94
Fort Humboldt, 65, 66, 167
Fort Jessup, 36, 38
Fort Sumter, 70
Fort Vancouver, 64, 65, 66
Fourteenth Amendment, 150
France, 170, 173
Fredericksburg, 104, 124, 128
Frémont, John C., 38, 68, 76, 79, 80, 84

Galena, 28, 69, 70, 72, 74, 80, 145, 177, 179, 180
Garfield, James A., 178, 179
Garland, John, 48-49, 50-51
Georgetown, Ohio, 7, 9, 11, 15, 17, 18, 28, 36, 46
Georgia, 109, 112, 117, 130, 131, 141
Germany, 169, 172

187

INDEX

Gettysburg, 108, 159
Golden Gate, 64
Gore, John, 62, 64
Gould, Jay, 151, 152, 155
Grant, Clara, 28
Grant, Elihu, 22
Grant, Ellen, 68
Grant, Frederick Dent, 62, 74, 105, 117-118, 119, 120, 147, 157, 158, 168, 173, 182
Grant, Hannah (née Simpson), 10-12, 18, 61, 147, 157
Grant, Hiram Ulysses, *see* Ulysses S. Grant
Grant, Jesse, 9, 10-20, 28, 60, 61, 67, 69, 147, 157, 158
Grant, Jesse Root, 68, 103, 121, 139, 147, 157, 158, 167, 172, 173
Grant, Julia (née Dent), 34, 37, 38, 39, 49-50, 59, 60-62, 65, 66, 67, 68, 69, 103, 105, 109, 113, 117, 118, 121, 132, 139, 140, 146, 147-148, 151, 152, 157-161, 164, 167, 170, 171, 172, 173-174, 177, 178, 179, 182, 183, 184
Grant, Mary Frances, 28
Grant, Matthew, 9
Grant, Nellie, 147, 157, 158, 160, 168, 170, 173, 179, 182
Grant, Noah, 9-10
Grant, Orvil, 28, 70
Grant, Simpson, 28
Grant, Ulysses S., boyhood of, 7-20; student at West Point, 21-31; at Jefferson Barracks, 33-37; and the Mexican War, 38-59; between Wars, 60-70; and the Civil War, 71-142; made full general, 143; and Andrew Johnson, 143-145; as President, 147-166; on world tour, 167-177; and the Republican convention, 1880, 178; in retirement, 179-183; death of, 183
Grant, Ulysses S., Jr., 65, 147, 157, 158, 161, 168, 172, 179, 180
Grant, Ulysses S., III, 66
Grant, Virginia, 28
Great Britain, 36, 46, 47, 153, 154-155, 168-169, 170

Greece, 171
Greeley, Horace, 156
Guadalupe Hidalgo, Treaty of, 59

Haiti, 153
Halleck, Henry Wager, 84, 86, 87, 92, 93-94, 98, 100-102, 103, 107, 110, 120, 127
Hamer, Tom L., 11, 17, 18-19, 46, 52
Harpers Ferry, 69, 134
Harris, Thomas, 75
Harrisburg, 21
Hayes, Rutherford B., 165, 167, 177, 179
Herrera, José, 41
Hoar, E. Rockwood, 149
Hood, John B., 131-132
Hooker, Joseph, 114, 115-116
Hoskins, John, 51
Hunter, David, 130

Illinois, 71, 74, 85
India, 173
Indiana, 167, 168
Ingalls, Rufus, 26, 64-65
Italy, 170, 171, 172

Jackson, 103, 106, 107, 109
Jackson, Andrew, 17
Jackson, Thomas J., "Stonewall," 29
James River, 129, 130
Japan, 175
Jefferson Barracks, 31, 33-37, 66, 144
Johnson, Andrew, 112, 141, 142, 143-145, 147, 149
Johnston, Albert S., 94, 96
Johnston, Joseph, 59, 106, 107, 120, 130, 132, 141, 184
Joseph, Franz, 172

Kaiser Wilhelm, 155, 169, 172
Kentucky, 9, 10, 15, 67, 78, 79, 80, 84, 85, 86, 92, 101, 109, 110
Knoxville, 110, 112, 117

Lee, Robert E., 26, 53, 54, 56, 59, 72, 94, 101, 107, 121, 123, 124-138

INDEX

Leopold, King, 169
Lincoln, Abraham, 70, 72, 76, 77, 84, 85, 92, 98, 104, 117, 118, 119, 120, 122, 130, 131, 132, 137, 139-141, 143, 154, 155
Lincoln, Robert, 141
Liverpool, 168
Logan, John A., 73
London, 169
Long Branch, 161, 179, 180
Longstreet, James, 25, 28, 33, 34, 40, 61, 109, 114, 138-139
Lookout Mountain, 112-113, 115, 116
Louisiana, 36, 37, 165
Louisiana Purchase, 9, 36
Louisville, 110, 111

McClellan, George B., 29, 54, 59, 72, 84, 88, 92, 93-94, 101, 103, 130
McClernand, John A., 73, 87, 89-91, 103, 106
McLean, Wilmer, 136
McPherson, James B., 106
Marshall, Charles, 136
Marshall, Johnny, 15, 20
Marshall, Margaret, 15
Maryland, 101, 149
Massachusetts, 9, 149
Matamoros, 42, 46, 48, 50
Maximilian, Archduke, 142-143
Maysville, 15, 17
Meade, George C., 108, 121, 123, 133, 134, 136, 138
Mediterranean, 170, 173
Memoirs, 19, 26, 42, 66, 75, 76, 181, 184
Memphis, 101, 102, 109
Mexico, 35-36, 41 42, 49, 58, 142-143, 153, 177
Mexico City, 36, 52, 53, 55, 56, 58, 59, 106
Mexican War, 42-59, 75, 76, 79, 128, 136-137, 153
Missionary Ridge, 112, 114, 115-117
Mississippi, 70
Mississippi River, 9, 74, 77, 78, 81-83, 85, 100, 102, 108, 120

Missouri, 29, 61, 74, 76, 77, 78, 81, 84
Mobile Bay, 131, 132
Monocacy, 174
Monroe Doctrine, 142
Monterrey, 47, 48, 49, 50, 52
Morris, Thomas, 18
Mount McGregor, 182-183

Napoleon III, 142
Nashville, 93, 94, 112, 117, 118, 121, 131
New Orleans, 9, 39, 102, 105, 106, 109, 110, 120
New York City, 21, 67, 162, 168, 179
New York *Herald,* 168, 170, 172
North Carolina, 132
Nueces River, 40, 42

Ohio, 7, 9, 36, 72, 85, 149, 165, 178
Ohio, 63
Ohio River, 9, 10, 67, 77, 79, 80, 112
Oregon, 36, 39, 46, 64, 65, 153, 165

Paducah, 78-79, 84, 87
Palo Alto, battle of, 44, 47, 52, 53, 75
Panama, 63
Paredes, Mariano, 41
Parker, Ely S., 137
Pemberton, John C., 102, 106-108, 132
Pennsylvania, 9, 21, 152
Petersburg, 129, 131, 133
Philadelphia, 21, 140, 149, 156, 162, 167, 179, 180
Pickett, George, 159
Pierce, Franklin, 68
Pillow, Gideon, 78, 79, 80, 81, 82, 89, 91
Pittsburgh, 9, 21
Point Isabel, 43, 45, 75
Point Pleasant, 9, 10, 11
Polk, James K., 39, 41, 46, 52
Port Hudson, 105, 106, 108, 109
Porter, David D., 105-106
Porter, Horace, 150, 159

189

INDEX

Portland, 64
Portugal, 172
Price, Sterling, 101
Pudget Sound, 155
Puebla, 55, 56

Rapidan River, 124, 126
Rawlins, John A., 70, 80-81, 83, 98, 132, 136, 145, 147, 149, 152, 163, 182
Reconstruction Act, 144, 150
Resaca de la Palma, battle of, 45, 47, 57
Richmond, 77, 108, 124, 127, 129, 130, 131, 133
Richmond, 173, 174, 175
Rio Grande, 42, 43, 45, 48, 52
Ripley, 18, 19, 20
River Queen, 132
Rosecrans, William S., 25, 102, 109-110, 111, 112
Russia, 153, 172

Sabine River, 38
St. Louis, 33, 34, 39, 61, 67, 68, 76, 92, 93, 99, 105, 109, 117, 118, 138, 165
St. Louis, 89
Samaná Bay, 153
San Antonio, 41
San Francisco, 64, 65, 67, 173, 176, 177
San Juan Islands, 155
Santo Domingo, 153-154
Sartoris, Algernon, 160, 168, 170
Scandinavia, 172
Scotland, 170
Scott, Winfield, 25, 38, 52-58, 72, 84, 106, 128
Scott, Winfield Hancock, 178
Sedgwick, John, 125
Seward, William H., 153
Seymour, Horatio, 145
Shenandoah, 154
Shenandoah Valley, 123-124, 130, 131, 132
Sheridan, Philip, 121, 131-134, 136, 142, 177, 182, 184

Sherman, John, 178
Sherman, William Tecumseh, 22-23, 25, 59, 68, 95-99, 103, 106, 109, 114, 115-117, 123, 130, 131-133, 141-142, 145, 165, 168, 182, 184
Shiloh, 94-99, 100, 125, 128, 181
Sigel, Franz, 123, 130
Slidell, John, 41
Smith, Charles F., 25, 79, 87, 89-91, 95
Smith, Kirby, 142
Smith, William Farrer, 113-114
Smithsonian Institution, 180
South Carolina, 70, 132, 165
Spain, 172
Spotsylvania, 127, 130
Stanley, Henry M., 171
Stanton, Edwin M., 110, 111, 119, 139, 142, 144
Stewart, A. T., 149
Suez Canal, 173, 174
Sumner, Charles, 153-154
Sutter's Mill, 64
Suviah, 40
Swett, Leonard, 84-85
Switzerland, 169-170

Taylor, Zachary, 38, 39, 41, 42-53, 58, 61, 68, 72
Tennessee, 85, 92, 94, 101, 102, 109, 112, 131
Tennessee River, 79, 85, 86, 87, 88, 112
Tenure of Office Act, 144
Texas, 35-36, 39, 40-42, 58, 120, 130, 142
Thayer, John, 89-91, 104
Thirteenth Amendment, 150
Thomas, George H., 25, 59, 110, 111-113, 115-116, 123, 131-132
Thomas, Lorenzo, 145
Tigress, 95, 96
Tilden, Samuel J., 165
Treaty of Washington, 154-155
Turkey, 171
Twain, Mark, 171, 181, 182
Tyler, John, 36

Union Pacific, 155

190

INDEX

United States Military Academy, see West Point

Vandalia, 170, 172
Vanderbilt, Cornelius, 180, 183
Veracruz, 52, 53, 54
Vicksburg, 102-108, 109, 132, 137, 181
Virginia, 72, 75, 77, 101
Vose, Josiah H., 33, 39

Wallace, Lew, 94, 96-97
Ward, Ferdinand, 172-173, 179-180
Washburne, Elihu B., 70, 77, 145, 149
Washington, George, 143
Washington, D.C., 19, 39, 107, 121, 130, 139, 140, 143, 145, 147, 161

Webster, Charles L., 181
West Point, 18-20, 21-31, 35, 38, 46, 53, 54, 56, 62, 64, 76, 79, 84, 123, 128, 138, 183, 184
Whiskey Ring, 164
Whistler, William, 39, 48, 61
White Haven, 34, 37, 38, 39, 60, 62, 67, 68, 179, 180
Wilderness, the, 124-127, 130, 181
Wilson, Henry, 156
Worth, William J., 50, 51, 57
Wright, Horatio, 127

Yates, Richard, 71, 72-73
Yellowstone National Park, 155
Young, John Russell, 168-169, 170, 172, 177

ABOUT THE AUTHORS

The collaboration of Bob and Jan Young began at the University of California at Los Angeles, where they met as undergraduates and found they shared a common interest in writing. Following their marriage in 1940, they spent most of the next ten years in the newspaper field. In 1950 they turned to freelance writing, concentrating first on the magazine field. In 1958 they published their first two books for children and now, after numerous other books, consider writing for young people their major interest.

Both are native Californians. Bob was born November 6, 1916 in Chico; attended Sacramento schools, UCLA and graduated from the University of Nevada. Jan was born March 6, 1919 in Lancaster; attended Pt. Loma and South Pasadena public schools and UCLA. They are the parents of four children. Their legal residence is in Ferndale on the redwood coast of northern California. Winters, they continue to spend in their former family home in Whittier in southern California.